The Daily Poet

Day-By-Day Prompts
For Your Writing Practice

Kelli Russell Agodon & Martha Silano

Two Sylvias Press

Two Sylvias Press
PO Box 1524
Kingston, WA 98346

Cover Design: Kelli Russell Agodon
Book Design: Annette Spaulding-Convy
Author Photo Credits: Rosendo Agodon and Langdon Cook

Thank you to the poets and their editors who have permitted Two Sylvias Press to use excerpts from previously published poems.

For more information on purchasing and/or downloading *The Daily Poet* and to learn more about Two Sylvias Press, please visit: www.twosylviaspress.com

ISBN: 1492706531
ISBN-13: 978-1492706533

for Gloria, Delaney, Marie, Alfred, Riley, and Ruby

Introduction

Art enables us to find ourselves and lose ourselves
at the same time. ~Thomas Merton

Dear Poet,

We created *The Daily Poet: Day-By-Day Prompts For Your Writing Practice* to help spark your creativity with 365 days of poetry-writing prompts. Each day offers a unique exercise to get you closer to a new poem.

As you begin this book of daily writing exercises, here's some helpful advice:

1) **There is no wrong way to complete a writing exercise.** Each exercise is designed to inspire and get you writing; this is our number one goal. If the exercise prompts you to write about a monkey and you write about a purple smoking jacket, or the time you lost a tooth on the train, that's wonderful. The goal is to write a poem a day, not feel bad your poem isn't following the exercise exactly.

2) **You don't have to begin January 1st.** You can start your year of writing on whatever day it is by beginning on that page/date. Or just start writing with January 1st as your first prompt. Our prompts follow the seasons, holidays, and

specific events that may have happened on that day in history, so you may want to complete the exercise for each specific day on the actual day, but you don't have to.

3) **You are welcome to read any poem we may have suggested before writing, but it's not a requirement.** Again, your main goal should be to simply write.

4) **Consider creating a word list to enhance and augment your daily writing.**
Throughout the day, write down interesting words you come across. Perhaps a neighbor said he was lollygagging. Or someone pointed out to you a specific kind of flower or bird—a lady's slipper or foxglove, a killdeer or ruby-throated hummingbird—write that down. Any words that may help inform or inspire your poems should be added to this ongoing list.

5) **Have fun.** Really, we created these exercises to help inspire you to write your best poems. Be as untamed and untethered as you like, letting your imagination run wild.

6) **If you get stuck, refer to Rule #1: There is no wrong way to do a writing exercise**...except to not write.

So enjoy, go forth, and write the poems you need to write. Our hope is that these exercises lead you to compose inventive, original, and downright daring poems, leaving you with a healthy stack of work that will enrich not only your life, but perhaps the lives of fellow readers.

Wishing you encouragement, bravery, and a daily motivational spark,

Kelli and Martha

JANUARY

JANUARY

1

· ·

New Year's Resolutions

Write a poem about a resolution you have never been able to keep. Or write a list poem of resolutions that would be ridiculously hard (or impossible!) to keep such as "Clean the windows of the Space Shuttle daily" or "Sweep the beach of all its sand." The more impossible the resolutions, the better!

JANUARY

2

. . . .

Protecting Niagara Falls

On this date in 1929, a document was signed between the US and Canada, protecting Niagara Falls from construction. Write a poem about something you want to protect. It can be a relationship, a memory, something in nature, or something in or about yourself. If this is a first person poem, allow the speaker to be vulnerable.

JANUARY

3

. . . .

Censored

In 1969, *Two Virgins,* by John Lennon and Yoko Ono, was confiscated at Newark Airport because the cover image depicts John and Yoko in the nude. Write down fifteen words you have never used in a poem, then write a poem using at least ten of those words, stretching the boundaries of what you feel comfortable writing about. If you find you are feeling self-conscious, remind yourself that you do not have to show this poem to anyone.

JANUARY

4

. . . .

I Hear It's Cold In Antarctica

Write a list of the coldest words you can think of—everything from ice to Ice Capades, snowball to Antarctica. Once you have your list of at least twenty words, incorporate the most interesting ones into a poem about summer, kite flying, or something else that has nothing to do with freezing temperatures.

JANUARY

5

. . . .

Vision Persona

Write a poem in the voice of someone other than yourself that offers a glimpse or hints at another possible outcome or future. Consider going back in history and writing about Abraham Lincoln deciding to stay home from yet another play, or write from the present about an event that has not yet happened or may never happen. For example, write from the point-of-view of snowboarders imagining all of the snow in the world has melted from global warming or someone preparing for an event (a wedding, an earthquake, a funeral, etc.) that may or may not actually happen. Allow history to rewrite itself or allow a new future for you or someone else to unfold.

JANUARY

6

. . . .

Stone Soup

Write a poem that begins with the image of a stone,
then add at least five of these words to it: kamikaze,
landslide, spill, bridge, vaccine, read, red, hollow,
mismatch, tilt, freeway, pillow, harmonica, fairy shrimp.
For extra credit, have the poem end with a soup image.

JANUARY

7

. . . .

Happiness And The A-Bomb

Compare your happiness to an atomic bomb or to something dangerous or frightening. How is your happiness the same as an atomic bomb? What images do you see if you were to imagine your happiness exploding in the desert? Think about all of the details related to the atomic bomb or something else dangerous, such as a tidal wave or tornado, and imagine your happiness about having those qualities. Allow the poem to be as realistic or surreal as you wish.

JANUARY

8

. . . .

Images By Listening

Close your eyes and listen to music that has no words. While you listen, what images come to mind? Allow your mind to go to all areas of the world, into your memories, and into all areas of time. Do certain instruments bring back childhood memories? Do certain sounds come with emotions—happy or sad, fear or confidence? Open your eyes and make a list of everything you saw. Use at least five of those images in a poem. If you are having trouble beginning, borrow the line, *I am skimming the edges...* from Kelli Russell Agodon's poem, "Yakima Ferry at Sunset."

JANUARY

9

. . . .

They Say It's Your Birthday

Today may not be your birthday, but write a birthday poem as if it is. The poem can either be to yourself on a specific birthday or to a friend as in "To Martha on Her Fortieth Birthday." Or if you just can't get into the birthday spirit, write a poem to or about Dave Matthews, Richard Nixon, Bob Denver (Gilligan on *Gilligan's Island*), or Joan Baez, and all who celebrate birthdays today.

JANUARY

10

. . . .

Alphabet Letter Of The Day

Choose a letter of the alphabet. Keeping a notebook with you, write down words that begin with your letter as you come into contact with them. If your letter is W and you are in the kitchen and you see a wine bottle, write down *wine bottle*. If your child comes in whining, write down *whining*. If you hear someone whistling, write that down. Keep writing until you have collected at least twenty-five words. Use at least fifteen of these words in a poem about something that does not start with the letter you chose.

JANUARY

11

. . . .

Surprise City

In 1949, Los Angeles documented its first recorded snowfall. Choose a city you are familiar with and write a poem about something you can't imagine happening there. It can relate to weather or be an event no one would expect. For example, you could write a poem in which all of Seattle's coffee shops go out of business and they begin selling steamed seawater. You could write a poem in which all New Yorkers wear flip-flops, or Las Vegas decides to turn off its lights Easter Weekend and instead offers an outside prayer service, or maybe Texas decides it's had enough of the cowboy hat and insists all ranchers now wear plaid berets. Use your imagination and see where your poem goes.

JANUARY

12

. . . .

Letter To An Artist

Write a poem addressed to an artist, living or dead. It can be an artist you admire or one whose work you do not particularly like. Do not feel you need to limit yourself to painters, as you are welcome to write a letter to any type of artist, including dancer Twyla Tharp, cellist Yo-Yo Ma, or cartoonist and creator of *The Simpsons*, Matt Groening. The poem can be to an artist in any field, including (but not limited to) literary, visual arts, dance, music, or performing arts.

JANUARY

13

. . . .

Every Explorer

On this day in 1610, Galileo Galilei discovered
Ganymede, the fourth moon of Jupiter. Write a poem
where you discover something and name it. It could be
moons of planets, a new type of flower, a new animal
species, a unique rock or mineral, or a new type of
music. Make the poem as funny or serious as you like
by creating whimsical silly names (such as the *Laizee*—a
new breed of French Poodle that hangs out on the
porch) or names that sound as if they fell out of a
scientific guide (such as a flower called the *iris vangoghus*
or the *cactus dontsithere*).

JANUARY

14

. . . .

Keep Running

Write a poem that is made up completely of one run-on
sentence. You can use commas, but no colons or semi-
colons. The poem can be on any topic you wish, but it
must be one complete sentence. If you're not sure how
to begin, start with the line, *S/he told me once...* Allow
the poem to wander through various scenes and details.
To keep the poem moving, use conjunctions like *and,
but, however*, and *although*.

JANUARY

15

· ·

The Rules

On this day in history in 1892, James Naismith (who is also credited for the first football helmet) published the rules for the sport of basketball. Write a poem made up of rules for something that does not yet have rules written for it. It could be "Rules for Wearing a Top Hat" or "Rules for Digging a Grave." Start by making a list of at least three activities that don't have rules, then choose one to focus on.

JANUARY

16

. . . .

Twenty Oil And Snow

Brainstorm ten words that come to mind when you think of snow and ten words that come to mind when you think of oil. Write a poem that uses a word from the "snow list" in the first line and a word from the "oil list" in the second line. Continue doing this until you have used all (or most) of the words.

JANUARY

17

· ·

A Life Worth Writing About

Write down three things you did yesterday. Think about the specific details of each event using all of the five senses: what you saw, heard, touched, smelled, and tasted. Choose one of these events to write a poem about. Or write one poem with three sections made up from each of the events.

JANUARY

18

A Sticky Situation

In 1919, twenty-one people were killed and one hundred fifty injured when a large molasses tank in Boston, Massachusetts, broke open and a wave of brown stickiness rushed through the streets. Write a poem that features an unusual death. The death or details of the event can be fictional or true.

JANUARY

19

· ·

The Legend Of Poe

Today is the birthday of Edgar Allan Poe. From 1949 to 2009, the "Poe Toaster," an unknown person, visited the grave of Edgar Allan Poe near midnight, leaving three roses and a half-filled bottle of cognac on Poe's grave. Make up a legend or strange story about a famous person or family member, and/or share a unique way to pay tribute to someone after he or she has died.

JANUARY

20

. . . .

Reoccurring Words And Dreams

Write a poem where the first word of a line begins with the same letter as the last word of the same line. Have the poem be about a reoccurring dream you have or had as a child. For example, the first line could be *My dream hinted at mailboxes* as *my* and *mailbox* both begin with the letter "m."

JANUARY

21

· ·

Use Some Sense

Instead of focusing predominantly on sight today, focus on taste, hearing, scent, and touch. As you notice something that doesn't involve sight, jot it down in a notebook. It could be "my hands smelled like pennies after digging through the change jar," or "heard a kingfisher calling over the sounds of waves." At the end of the day, write a poem using your jotted down images.

JANUARY

22

. . . .

Couplet Lost

Write a poem that has only two lines (no more than
thirteen syllables each). End the poem with an image
of something being lost. Give the poem either a long
or one-word title.

JANUARY

23

· ·

Titling Dali

On this day in 1989, Salvador Dali died at age eighty-four in Spain. Write a poem with the title of one of Dali's paintings or use four of these titles from his works in a poem: *Self-Portrait in the Studio, The Artist's Father at Llane Beach, Coffee House Scene in Madrid, Fried Egg on the Plate without the Plate, Honey Is Sweeter Than Blood, Man with Unhealthy Complexion Listening to the Sound of the Sea, The Invisible Harp, West Side of the Isle of the Dead, A Couple with Their Heads Full of Clouds, Two Pieces of Bread, Expressing the Sentiment of Love, Cathedral of Thumbs, Soft Monster.*

JANUARY

24

. . . .

Twin Form

Write a poem about twins where the first and last lines
are the same line. Have the poem be about two of
something or two similar events. As you continue to
write, consider objects that come in pairs or images that
have something to do with twins (Doublemint gum,
pairs of socks, hot and cold faucet handles, etc.). Write
your poem in couplets or have stanzas mirror each
other, such as two stanzas of three lines, then two
stanzas of five lines. Feel free to title the poem "Twins"
even if your poem isn't directly about two people.

JANUARY

25

. . . .

I Abstractly Love Your Concreteness

Choose an abstract word such as *love, hate, obsession, freedom, success*, etc. for your title, then write a poem that is made up completely of concrete images. For example, if I chose the word "Love" for my title, I might use images such as two robins on the branch of a cherry tree or the heart of a cinnamon roll. Alternatively, if I chose the word "Shame," I might use images such as a bus stop covered in vines or a child walking away. Don't feel you need to be completely literal—allow for a little mystery, letting your images do the work for you.

JANUARY

26

. . . .

Large To Small

Write a poem that begins with a very large image, such as the universe at night, Earth, a country, an ocean, Jupiter, a continent, a cargo ship, or some other gargantuan object. Then, throughout your poem, have each image following become smaller than the previous one. Write until you arrive at the tiniest of images, and end your poem there.

JANUARY

27

· ·

Journalistic Inspiration

Find an interesting newspaper article and circle all of the words that interest you. Write a poem about a topic that has nothing to do with the article. See if you can use these words in new ways. If the article was about the environment and you circled the words "fracking" and "global warming" think about new ways that you can use these terms, such as "fracking one's heart" or "having global warming of the brain." See where your poem leads you.

JANUARY

28

. . . .

Splatterings And Drippings

Today is the birthday of painter Jackson Pollock. Pollock was well-known for his drip paintings, where he would splash many colors of paint onto large canvases he had placed on the floor. Write a poem inspired by this style of painting or by the wild style of a Pollock painting. Maybe dribble words across the page or splatter one color throughout your poem. Or write an ekphrastic poem (an ekphrastic poem describes, comments on, and or dramatizes a work or works of visual art) about one of his paintings or a unique image you see in it.

JANUARY

29

· ·

Twitter Me This

Write a "Twitter poem"—a poem where each stanza is a complete thought or sentence not more than 140 characters in length. To keep with this Twitter theme, have each stanza be about a unique topic not related to the stanza above or below it.

JANUARY

30

· ·

Overheard Poetry

Spend a few minutes eavesdropping on a conversation today. Make sure to have your notebook with you while you listen, writing down exact quotes. Use these notes to write a poem with the conversation, lines, or images you heard woven into it. The poem can be about the conversation the people were having or a completely different topic. If you are not near anyone today, think about a conversation you once had or make something up.

JANUARY

31

. . . .

Yet Another Sticky Situation

In 1930, Scotch Tape was invented. Write a poem about a sticky situation you or someone you know has been in. Make sure to be specific with details and images. Once the poem is completed, cut up the poem into individual lines and use scotch tape to tape it back together, but in a *different* order.

FEBRUARY

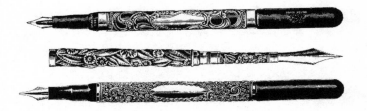

FEBRUARY

1

. . . .

Dreaming Of Langston Hughes

It's the birthday of Langston Hughes, born in 1902. In the spirit of Hughes, read his poem "A Dream Deferred" and write your own metaphoric and rhymed poem that both asks and answers questions. For example, you might ask: *What happens to a vacation deferred?* or *What happens to a remodel deferred?* Hughes' dream festers like a sore. What will your long-lost vacation or remodel do?

FEBRUARY

2

· ·

Starting Over

Imagine that you are given the chance to start your life over. In this new life you can choose your parents, your hometown, your travels, and your educational and/or career paths, along with your partner, children (or lack thereof), and friends. What would you change about your life so far if you could? Write a poem that shares about this new, alternate life.

FEBRUARY

3

. . . .

Money Changes Everything

On this date in 1690, the Massachusetts Bay Company issued the first paper money. Write a poem that involves the exchange of currency for goods. To get you started, consider these facts: President Andrew Johnson purchased the Louisiana Territory for three cents an acre. The local Indians gave Peter Minuit the island of Manhattan in exchange for some hatchets, cloth, and beads with an approximate worth of sixty guilders (the equivalent of 1 ½ pounds of silver). Feel free to use any of these facts or consider any strange things you have spent money on and write about that.

FEBRUARY

4

· ·

The Language Of Facebook

On this date in 2004, Mark Zuckerberg founded
Facebook. Write a poem that incorporates one or more
of these social networking-inspired coinages: LOL
(Laughing Out Loud), OMG (Oh My Gosh), IMHO
(In My Humble Opinion), facebragging, vaguebooking,
unfriend, Tweetup, lappy (laptop), smartphone, <3. If
you need an opening line, browse through your old
Facebook statuses and choose one with which to begin
your poem.

FEBRUARY

5

. . . .

Jokes And Laughs

In celebration of the first *Reader's Digest* publication on this date in 1922, head to the *Reader's Digest* home page and click on *Jokes*: http://www.rd.com/jokes. After reading several jokes, draft a poem that riffs on scenarios and punchlines that most intrigue you. Alternatively, write a poem of three or four sections in which each section begins with a well-known riddle. Examples: What time is it when an elephant sits on a fence? What's black and white and red all over? Why did the chicken cross the road?

FEBRUARY

6

. . . .

Integrated Circuit

On this date in 1959, Jack Kilby of Texas Instruments filed the first patent for an integrated circuit. In honor of all things microchipped, write a poem in the voice of a stereotypical 1950s American housewife as she puzzles over circuit diagrams and contemplates possible uses for this new invention.

FEBRUARY

7

. . . .

Labor-Saving Device

In honor of the birthday of John Deere, inventor of the steel plow, write a poem about your favorite labor saving device Examples: coffee grinder/maker, ice maker, electric can opener, vacuum cleaner, washing machine, etc. Bonus source: consult the user manual of your chosen device.

FEBRUARY

8

. . . .

Under Elizabeth Bishop's Spell

It's the birthday of Elizabeth Bishop, one of the most well-regarded poets of the 20th century. Bishop's forte is looking closely at the world's creatures and sharing them with her reader in a painterly fashion: palm trees are fistfuls of limp fish-skeletons and a dead hen's wing is as thin as tissue paper. For today's poem, take a walk around your block and notice the small and seemingly insignificant things you pass (a leaf, a beetle, a patch of poppies), as well as your neighbors and/or their dogs, cats, and children. If you are up for it, take notes. Either way, return to your desk to describe in vivid detail what you observed.

FEBRUARY

9

. . . .

Incremental

Compose a poem of address that begins with one word (the person, place, or thing being addressed), and then progresses by adding one word to the length of each line (for example: line 1 is one word long, line 2 is two words long, line 3 is three words long, etc.). Aim for a poem of at least ten lines.

FEBRUARY

10

. . . .

Get Thee To A Library

Spend some time doing a little research today. Possible
subjects: Egyptian pharaohs, astronomy, reptiles,
geologic features of South America. Incorporate lesser-
known facts about your chosen subject into your poem.
If you are nowhere near a library and don't have
Internet, write a poem on a subject you know little or
nothing about, making up facts as you please.

FEBRUARY

11

. . . .

Dream Weaver

Write a poem about a recurring nightmare. Do not begin your poem "In the dream," but instead, launch straight into the telling: "My parents and I were driving from Kentucky to New Jersey, but suddenly the car veered left, and I was on a roller coaster made of Jello." For more inspiration, read some of Charles Simic's poems to get yourself in a surreal mood.

FEBRUARY

12

· ·

Abraham Lincoln

Today is the birthday of Abraham Lincoln, the sixteenth president of the United States. Lincoln is said to have stated that "Those who deny freedom to others, deserve it not themselves." For today's exercise, write a poem that includes someone or something being set free. Examples: a zoo animal, a caged chicken, a tethered dog, a human being (either you or someone you know).

FEBRUARY

13

· ·

Synonym / Antonym

Choose a word and its antonym then write a poem that contrasts the two extremes. Consult a dictionary or thesaurus to find all the synonyms for your opposite words, or simply rely on memory to construct your lists of opposites. Pairing possibilities:

bright/dim
light/heavy
large/small
extrovert/introvert

FEBRUARY

14

. . . .

Be Mine

Relying on memory, a culinary dictionary, or a stack of
cookbooks, make three separate lists of verbs, nouns,
and adjectives related to cooking and baking (*score, truss,
whisk, juice*), then write a love poem using at least five
words from each list.

FEBRUARY

15

. . . .

Liar, Liar, Pants On Fire

Write a poem in which not a single word is true. The poem may consist of lies about yourself, or it could focus on fabricated historical events, laws of physics, or geographic wonders. Let your imagination run toward the false!

FEBRUARY

16

. . . .

Shadow

Begin writing a poem about your shadow, but don't
stop there. Describe the shadows of what you see
around you: robins, sheds, skyscrapers, park benches,
soda pop cans. If you want, take it a step farther,
describing the shadow your father casts upon you or
your shadow self.

FEBRUARY

17

∙ ∙

Winter

Start by making a list of memories you associate with winter. Describe your childhood sled or saucer, your favorite skating pond or tobogganing hill. Did you go on ski vacations, or was winter more a time for hunkering down in a warm house? What does winter smell like? Taste like? Describe your favorite winter outfit. Take these memory snippets and fashion them into a wintry poem.

FEBRUARY

18

. . . .

Still Gray

Write a poem in the key of gray. Begin by looking up synonyms for gray. Examples: ashen, argentine, leaden, pewter, slate, hoary. Gray is also associated with cheerlessness, depression, and dreariness. Write a poem that strikes a dismal, dreary tone, or write a poem that uses synonyms for gray about a joyful topic.

FEBRUARY

19

· ·

Obsolete

On this date in 1878, Thomas Edison received a patent for the phonograph. Write a poem about a once-common household item that is now obsolete. Examples: transistor radio, cassette recorder, 8-track player, modem, oscilloscope, typewriter, Polaroid instant camera, Walkman.

FEBRUARY

20

. . . .

Directions

Use the following line from Natasha Tretheway's
"Theories of Time and Space" to begin a poem that
provides directions to a specific geographic place:
Everywhere you go will be somewhere / you've never been. Aim
to engage all five of your reader's senses as you lead
him or her to Crater Lake, Munich, Tasmania, Italy, the
Grand Canyon, etc.

FEBRUARY

21

. . . .

Poem Of Address

Write a poem of address to someone or something that
angers you. It might be a former lover, a pair of shoes
that gave you blisters, or the mosquito that buzzed in
your ear all night. Extra credit: employ a 6-line stanza
and an AABBCC rhyme scheme in each stanza.

FEBRUARY

22

. . . .

Washington's Birthday

On this date in 1732, George Washington was born. Head to the Metropolitan Museum website (http://www.metmuseum.org) and study closely the painting titled *Washington Crossing the Delaware* (you can find the painting here: http://www.metmuseum.org/Collections/search-the-collections/20011777).

Zoom in on General Washington's face, the icy Delaware, the billowing American flag, then write a poem that describes the scene and/or shares historical facts about the December 26, 1776 attack on the Hessians near Trenton, New Jersey. If you do not have Internet access, use the portrait of Washington's face on the American dollar or quarter to inspire a poem about the ubiquity of Washington's face in American culture.

FEBRUARY

23

. . . .

Sonnet In Four Sentences

Today is the birthday of Edna St. Vincent Millay. She is known for her passionate sonnets, including the much-anthologized, "Love is Not All." In honor of this particular sonnet by Millay, write a sonnet of four long sentences—the first sentence ending at line 8, the second at line 13, and the third and fourth sentences both in line 14. In your sonnet, include at least four of the following words: compare, hot, eye, star, ground, change, strong. Millay's original sonnet, "Love is Not All," can be viewed at:

http://www.poets.org/viewmedia.php/prmMID/23297.

FEBRUARY

24

. . . .

If You Could Be Anybody

Write a poem that answers the question "If you could be anybody, who would you be?" You may have one or more answers to this question—feel free to make this a list poem. Here is an example from Martha Silano's "If You Could Be Anybody, Who Would You Be?":
Thomas Edison / on the day he invented the phonograph— telegraph tape, set at high speed, / emitting human speech. Paper speaking!

FEBRUARY

25

. . . .

Time Travel

If you could enter a time machine and return to another era or epoch, which one would you choose and, more importantly, why? After doing a bit of research on your chosen era, write a poem that takes the reader by the hand and leads him or her on a journey through another time and place.

FEBRUARY

26

. . . .

Just Like A Prayer

In the manner of William Butler Yeats' poem "Prayer for My Daughter," (which can be found here: http://www.poetryfoundation.org/poetrymagazine/poem/3838), write a poem to a relative or friend in the form of a prayer. What do you wish for your chosen recipient? Yeats describes a howling storm; describe the weather at your location. Is the relative nearby? What is the speaker's mental state? Share images using all of your senses; flood your poem with metaphor. Example: *May she become a flourishing hidden tree.*

FEBRUARY

27

. . . .

Anaphora

A type of parallelism created when successive lines begin with the same word or phrase, anaphora is one of the world's oldest writing techniques, creating a driving rhythm that intensifies emotion. Great examples of anaphoric poems include Mark Strand's "From a Litany," Whitman's "Out of the Cradle Endlessly Rocking," and Joel Brainard's *I Remember,* an entire book of poems in which every line begins *I remember.* Choose a word or phrase and repeat it at the beginning of every line of your own poem.

FEBRUARY

28

. . . .

Vice

"It has been my experience that folks who have no vices have very few virtues," said Abraham Lincoln. Write a poem detailing your vices or past vices. Maybe you purchase illegal fireworks or run red lights. Maybe you smoke or have smoked in the past. Maybe you have a secret relationship with gummy bears after your kids go to sleep, or you throw away pennies because you hate keeping them in your wallet. In what way or ways do your vices enable you to be virtuous?

FEBRUARY

29

. . . .

Leaping

In honor of leap year, draft a descriptive poem that leaps from image to image. As you revise, infuse your poem with passion and aliveness, then take it a step further, pushing toward surrealist free-association. Whether you are describing a mushroom or a drive to the country, your goal is to make the ordinary fresh and unusual. Examples: water kneels, lamplight falls on all fours, cornfields breath.

MARCH

1

. . . .

Another Way To Be Faithful

On this day in 1872, Congress authorized the creation of Yellowstone National Park. Since one of the most famous American natural landmarks is the geyser, "Old Faithful," write a poem entitled "Old Faithful" that has nothing to do with Yellowstone Park *or* geysers. Think about what in your life has been faithful to you: a relationship, a car, an illness, a pet, a pen, a roof that survived a bad windstorm. The more peculiar the item is, the more interesting the poem will be.

MARCH

2

. . . .

One Fish, Two Fish, Red Fish, Blue Fish

Theodore Seuss Geisel, known better as "Dr. Seuss," was born on this day in 1904. Write a poem that mentions at least one character from your favorite Dr. Seuss story: Horton, the Lorax, the Grinch, Sam-I-Am, Thing 1 and Thing 2, Yertle the Turtle, etc. Or, write a poem using images from his stories: green eggs and ham, bears on unicycles, etc.

MARCH

3

Sugarbeep, I Love You

Write a poem where you take two very different words and put them together to make a new word. For example, "tickle" and "lagoon" become "ticklelagoon" or "cabbage" and "joy" make "cabbagejoy." Now use these new, unique words to create a poem. If you're having trouble thinking of words, grab the nearest book or dictionary and just flip open to any page and see what words you find.

MARCH

4

. . . .

You Look Like Marilyn Monroe, Except In The Eyes

In 1997, President Bill Clinton barred spending any federal money on human cloning, but this doesn't mean your poem can't include a clone or two. Write a poem where you clone a famous person or yourself. How are they different in your poem? What are some things they do as clones that they wouldn't do in real life? Could you write a poem with many famous clones bumping into each other? Or what if you cloned yourself and sent her/him out into the world: what would the clone-you learn? Let your imagination go wild on this one, aiming to take your poem as far as you can into its make-believe world.

MARCH

5

· ·

Midnight And You're Awake

In the poem "Nocturne," Susan Rich writes: *I take my place in the insomniac's village.* Write a poem about a time you were awake in the middle of the night—what you discovered about the world when everyone was sleeping, or what you learned about yourself. If you can't remember a specific incident, make one up. You might imagine being awake at midnight and hearing a raccoon on your porch, or pretending you are looking off your balcony in the city and you see two people kissing. What happens in the world when most people are asleep? Write a poem that surprises the reader with what s/he is missing.

MARCH

6

. . . .

I Prefer Chocolate Chip

In 1912, Nabisco introduced Oreo cookies, and since then, they've become the bestselling cookie of all time. Write a poem about your favorite cookie or about the Oreo. Have your cookie appear where you don't imagine cookies—eat a cookie while waterskiing or taking a bath, eat an Oreo at a black-tie event, or a have a stranger offer you a cookie on the subway. Feel free to use the names of more than one cookie or dessert, such as macaroon, shortbread, animal crackers, etc. To provide inspiration, snack on cookies while you write.

MARCH

7

. . . .

Let It Break

In the poem, "For practice, let something stay broken,"
Molly Tenenbaum writes, *the faucet's drip keeps you waking.*
Write a poem about something that's broken, whether a
relationship or an item in your house. What lessons can
you discover from this broken item? If you can't think
of anything broken, find something in your home you
don't need—like a chipped plate, a paperclip, a
scratched frame—and break it. Write about the
experience of breaking a material item and the details of
the moment, including how it felt, what it sounded like
when it broke, what it looked like in its brokenness.

MARCH

8

· ·

Where Have You Gone, Joe DiMaggio?

On this date in 1999, baseball legend Joe DiMaggio died at the age of eighty-four. Think about that iconic line and question, *Where have you gone, Joe DiMaggio?* from the Simon & Garfunkel song "Mrs. Robinson," and write a poem that addresses it. Does Joe DiMaggio meet up with Marilyn Monroe in heaven? Does his spirit remain alive in the threads of his New York Yankees uniform? Let the poem explore a specific memory you have with baseball, and let Joltin' Joe wander into it. If you're not familiar with Joe DiMaggio, do a little research and see if you can find an unusual fact about him to include in your poem.

MARCH

9

. . . .

Oh, God!

On this day in 1996, comedian George Burns, who played a cigar-smoking God in the movie *Oh, God!*, died. Write a poem where God or any Supreme Being (from a religion or mythological) is doing something you don't expect him/her to do. Maybe God is not only a creator, but a comedian. Maybe this Supreme Being has signed up for a Facebook account. Maybe God wants to visit the Rock and Roll Hall of Fame. This is another exercise where your imagination and the peculiarity and specific details in your poem will strengthen your work.

MARCH

10

. . . .

Choose Your Own Odd Couple

On this day in 1965, Neil Simon's play, *The Odd Couple*, debuted. Write a poem in which two famous people you wouldn't expect to see together interact. The people can be dead, living, or fictional. Think Frida Kahlo having a conversation with Bugs Bunny, or Elvis Presley doing a crossword puzzle with Elvis Costello. Feel free to use any two people or characters one would never expect to see together. Put them in a poem and see what they do.

MARCH

11

. . . .

Deja Vu

Write a poem about a déjà vu experience. To strengthen that "I've been here before" feeling and allow your reader to experience it with you, repeat words and images from the first stanza in the stanzas that follow. If you don't know how to begin, start with *I walked into a room I had already walked into before*... and see where it takes you.

MARCH

12

. . . .

A Guide To Life

In 1912, the Girl Guides, forerunner to the Girl Scouts of America, began. Using skills you learned from Girl Scouts, Camp Fire Girls, or the Boy Scouts, create a poem about modern life. For example, riff on the Boy Scout motto "Be Prepared" and what it means for you today. Always having your cellphone charged? Always knowing where your car keys are? If you were never a scout or know little about camping, feel free to research the details of these clubs, their handbooks, and guides. Use specific references as you write your poem.

MARCH

13

. . . .

Wish

Write a poem in three stanzas that explores three unique wishes. To keep this poem interesting, make sure stanza one mentions a dessert, stanza two refers to a famous dead person, and stanza three includes a kind of tool. Your wishes can be whatever you like, but make sure somewhere in the stanza these three requirements are met.

MARCH

14

. . . .

Sylvia Beach And
Shakespeare & Co.

On this day in 1887, Sylvia Beach, founder of the American bookstore in Paris called Shakespeare & Co., was born. Sylvia loved writers and helped them (including James Joyce) get published. Write a poem that explores a relationship that takes place in a bookstore. Make sure to use details from the bookstore—the scent and feel of the books, the sound of the other customers, the cash register, etc. Your poem can be set in the present or far in the past; but the entire scene should take place in a bookstore.

MARCH

15

· ·

Meandering To The Answer

Write a poem that begins with a difficult question and ends with an answer. Let the poem meander through different subjects that have nothing to do with the question or the answer. Allow your brain to write in almost a stream-of-consciousness way until you can tie in the answer at the end. And if you can't come up with an answer, that's okay, too, just refer back to the original question, perhaps with an image, and end the poem there.

MARCH

16

. . . .

Periwinkle K

On this day in 1850, Nathaniel Hawthorne published *The Scarlet Letter.* To give a nod to this book, choose a letter of the alphabet plus an interesting color, and write a poem where the color and the letter repeat throughout. The poem can be about anything, but you're welcome to make it scandalous, perhaps about an affair.

MARCH

17

. . . .

The Luck Of The Irish

To celebrate St. Patrick's Day, write a poem about Ireland or something Irish. It can be Delaney's Bar or the Book of Kells, Guinness beer or a Celtic cross. If you're Irish yourself, explore your own heritage. But even if you're not Irish, make sure to include images of Ireland or Irish culture. You can start the poem with the line, *The last time I was in Ireland* or *I've never been to Ireland, but. . .*

MARCH

18

· ·

A Poem About Nothing

In a memorable *Seinfeld* episode, it's proclaimed that *Seinfeld* is "a show about nothing." Of course, everything is about something, so for this exercise, write a poem about nothing—a poem where nothing fantastic happens. Make sure to focus on the particulars of this regular day where nothing out of the usual happens. Focusing on the specific details will help to ensure that your poem connects with its audience.

MARCH

19

· ·

Gamble Your Life Away

On this day in 1931, Nevada legalized gambling. Write a poem that explores gambling. Allow that topic to extend into relationships—what have you gambled away or what (or whom) have you bet on and lost? Feel free to mention slot machines, roulette, poker, or any words that relate to gambling. Alternatively, write about something you've won or lost, or a poem on the theme of "what happens in Vegas, stays in Vegas." Maybe you took a risk in your life and something good (or bad) happened. Let the glitter and lights of Las Vegas decorate your poem as needed.

MARCH

20

. . . .

The Yoko Factor

On this day in 1969, John Lennon married Yoko Ono. Some believe their union led to the break-up of the Beatles, while others focus on their inspiring love. Write a poem that celebrates the beauty of something that goes on to cause injury to others—maybe it's the great Chicago fire, how beautifully it lit up the sky, or the eye of the hurricane and the amazing ability of nature to create incredible force with a calmness at its center. You are also welcome to write about the beauty of something painful, a love relationship broken up by violence, as in John and Yoko's romance, cut short in 1980 by John's murder. Whatever it is, find the beauty in it, no matter how small (or large).

MARCH

21

. . . .

Save Ferris

In honor of Matthew Broderick's birthday, (the star of
the eighties flick, *Ferris Bueller's Day Off*) write a poem
about playing hooky from work, school, or life. Have
the speaker do something s/he wouldn't normally do—
kiss a stranger, splurge on something unique, ride a
motorcycle, or give flowers to a stranger. Allow magical
things to happen—synchronicities or coincidences. For
extra credit, reference the song "Danke Schoen" or
"Twist and Shout."

MARCH

22

. . . .

Many Lies And One Truth

Write a poem where every line but one is a lie. See what amazing stories you can make up, then offer one interesting thing that actually happened to you. Allow yourself to be as creative as you can without sounding as if you're lying. For example, instead of saying, "I was once a movie star" maybe write that you were an extra in the movie *Forrest Gump*. Remember to include specific details in your lies so they seem more realistic.

MARCH

23

. . . .

Starlets

On this day in 1908, Joan Crawford was born and, in 2011, Elizabeth Taylor died. To honor these movie stars, write a poem that references one of their movies or one of their characteristics. Consider writing about *What Ever Happened to Baby Jane?*, *Johnny Guitar*, *Cleopatra*, *Who's Afraid of Virginia Woolf?*, or *Cat on a Hot Tin Roof.* Maybe your poem will mention violet eyes or thick eyebrows. Whatever you choose, write a poem that returns us to another era of Hollywood glamour, or write a poem about the Hollywood of today that references the past.

MARCH

24

. . . .

The Magician's Tricks

On this day in 1874, magician Harry Houdini was born. Write a poem about a magician's trick or a poem where you are the magician or magician's assistant. Think of all the details that make up a magic show—the bunny in the hat, the doves, the sawing in half of a body, the lights, the smoke, the effects—and include your favorite details in your poem.

MARCH

25

. . . .

Opposite Day At Sunset

Write a poem about watching the sunset with a lover or a favorite person. Capture all the details of the moment—what you talked about, how you felt, the look of the landscape. Next return to the poem and revise it so every other adjective or noun is the opposite of what you wrote. Does doing this make your poem more interesting or surprising? Finally, revise the poem again, keeping the opposite words you like, and changing the ones that you don't like back to what they were or to something better.

MARCH

26

. . . .

Whitman Chocolates

Walt Whitman died on this day in 1892. Read some of Walt Whitman's poems, then write a poem in his style about a box of chocolates. Try not to take this too seriously; but simply allow your Whitman poem to flow onto the page. If you get stuck, read another one of his poems, striving to copy his tone, style, use of repetition, and/or imagery.

MARCH

27

. . . .

The Numbers Have It

Make a list of favorite numbers and mathematical terms, such as *divide, equals, plus, subtract, minus, equation, algebra,* etc. Write a poem about a personal experience while traveling. Make sure the experience doesn't have anything to do with math or numbers, but use the numbers and terms in a way that may be surprising to your reader—*the taxi cab equaled a trip to the part of town where no one goes; she was an awkward equation; she divided up her heart and left a blank spot for X; she packed her three hearts and eighty reasons to stay.*

MARCH

28

. . . .

Underwater

On this day in 1941, novelist Virginia Woolf committed suicide by placing stones in a pocket of her coat and walking into the Ouse River in Sussex. Write a poem that explores a drowning or near drowning. It can be based on a true story or be entirely fictional. If you're having trouble with the beginning, consider starting the poem with the image of floating or being underwater.

MARCH

29

· ·

Sacred Past

Make a list of ten things you hold sacred. It could be a drawing by your child, your grandmother's wedding ring, or a special memory you have. Write a poem where you find each of these three items while walking through your current or childhood home. Try not to be sentimental about the items, but allow these things that you hold sacred to tell a story of your past or that of someone else.

MARCH

30

. . . .

Our Love's In Jeopardy

On this day in 1964, the game show *Jeopardy* premiered
on television. The show is not like other games shows
in that host Alex Trebek reads the *answers* for certain
topics and the contestants have to guess what the
question is. Write a poem made up entirely of seven
questions about a love relationship gone awry (or
another topic that's been on your mind), or write a
poem made up of seven answers you imagine an ex-
lover would give you if you asked him or her a specific
question: "Why did you leave me?" or "Where did we
go wrong?"

MARCH

31

. . . .

Surprise Party For Mom

Write a poem about your mother or someone who has been like a mother to you. To keep this poem from being sentimental, write about a time when you discovered something about her that surprised you, for instance, maybe you found a photo of her in a revealing outfit or learned that as a teenager, she was hired to perform as a mermaid at a Florida tourist attraction. Allow the poem to move from something surprising about her into something surprising about yourself. Make sure not to "wrap up" the poem at the end, but allow the reader to make his/her own connections between the two surprises.

APRIL

APRIL

1

· ·

April Fool's

Write a poem that contains the linguistic equivalent of a rubber mouse in the fridge or a plastic cockroach on the kitchen counter. In other words, let today's poem surprise your reader with an arresting extended metaphor—*I am a blue tree...* or an unexpected subject or situation. The goal of this poem is to startle. See how many ways you can foist the unexpected on your reader and yourself.

APRIL

2

. . . .

Collage

Write a poem that works in much the same way a visual collage works: juxtaposing unlikely images and facts. For example, your poem might combine the following subjects: Nicoise olives, subatomic particles, the language of marriage certificates, beetles, ukuleles. Your poem may or may not find a common thread among its disparate parts.

APRIL

3

. . . .

Concrete

In honor of George Herbert, born this day in 1593, and author of "Easter Wings" (written in the shape of two sets of wings), write a poem about a specific thing in the shape of that object. Examples: an apple, a snake, a flower, a rocket ship, a hat. Be as creative as you wish.

APRIL

4

∙ ∙

Notebook

Go through your own or someone else's notebook, mining interesting snippets for today's poem. If you don't have a notebook at hand, grab a newspaper or magazine and see what you find. You can also check out the following books: *Straw for the Fire: From the Notebooks of Theodore Roethke, Susan Sontag Reborn: Journals & Notebooks: 1947-1963,* Charles Simic's *The Monster Loves His Labyrinth: Notebooks.*

APRIL

5

· ·

I Remember

Write a poem in which every line begins with the words *I remember...* Here are some sample lines to help inspire you: *I remember the giant Modess sign on the lawn where we watched fireworks / I remember asking my mother "what's a tampon?" (she did not answer).* For further inspiration, check out Joe Brainard's book, *I Remember.* Aim to use fresh, personal, and unexpected language in your poem as you repeat *I remember* at the opening of every line.

APRIL

6

. . . .

Skate-Away

Write a poem in celebration of Isaac Hodgson's 1869 patent for roller skates in one of three ways: (1) write a poem about your own roller skating memories, (2) watch some videos of roller skaters and write a descriptive poem based on your viewing, (3) write about a time you were metaphorically off-balance but determined to push forward.

APRIL

7

· ·

Backwards Acrostic

Write a poem in which the final letter of each line spells out a word, quotation, name, or a line from a favorite poem. The poem you create may or may not have to do directly with the subject of your chosen word or set of words.

APRIL

8

· ·

Let's Escape

In honor of the first fire escape created on this date in 1766 (a wicker basket on a pulley with a chain), write a poem in which someone or something is fleeing to safety. Suggestions: a grasshopper fleeing a kestrel or a victim of violence fleeing his or her assailant.

APRIL

9

. . . .

Deprivation vs. Plentitude

Write a poem in which hard times (unemployment, staycations, soup kitchens, frugality, thrift store shopping, in the red), are contrasted with financially stable times (employment, consumerism, vacations, lavish gift giving, in the black). Write your poem in couplets, alternating a line of deprivation with a line of plentitude, as in the example: *At Goodwill she slipped her foot into the least scuffed-up Mary Jane, dreaming of the days of shiny new stilettos...*

APRIL

10

· ·

Only Fasten

On this date in 1849, Walter Hunt received a patent for the spring safety pin. Write a poem that uses at least seven of these words: adhere, affix, anchor, attach, bind, bolt, bond, brace, catch, cohere, connect, couple, glue, hitch, hold, hook, knot, latch, united.

APRIL

11

. . . .

Virtue Comes To Visit

For today's poem put yourself in this scenario: a saint or wisdom figure (choose a favorite: Francis of Assisi, Buddha, Teresa of Avila, Moses, Voltaire, Kwan Yin, etc.) knocks on your door. What do you ask or tell him or her? What words of wisdom, if any, does s/he leave you with? Don't question what comes to mind. Write it all down and revise your poem later.

APRIL

12

. . . .

Blissful And Miraculous

Write a poem that begins *In Bliss, Idaho, at the Miracle Hot Springs...* What might happen to a speaker in such a place? Perhaps she finds true happiness and witnesses divine grace, but she might just as easily encounter obstacles that prevent either, such as a mosquito swarm or throngs of tourists wearing Snoopy t-shirts. Share all the quirky details with your reader.

APRIL

13

. . . .

Digging For Dirt

In honor of Seamus Heaney's birthday (b. 1939), write a poem about your native land, providing historical details without being overtly political. Instead, focus on personal details about, for instance, what your parents and/or grandparents did for a living. Be present in your poem, and don't shy away from unlikely ("ordinary") poetic subjects, such as digging in the dirt, farming, baking or cleaning the house.

APRIL

14

. . . .

After The Rain

Write a poem that begins: *After the rain it all looked different.* Make sure your poem contains specific details about the landscape, the glistening, the spring flowers, and perhaps the mood of the speaker.

APRIL

15

. . . .

Mr. Da Vinci's Art

In honor of Leonardo da Vinci's birthday on this date
in 1452, write an ekphrastic poem about one of his
masterpieces or journal sketches. *Ekphrastic* derives
from the Greek *ekphrazein*, meaning to recount, to
describe + to explain. An ekphrastic poem describes,
comments on, and or dramatizes a work or works of
visual art. For today's poem, write your ekphrastic
poem in the voice of someone or something depicted in
da Vinci's paintings or sketches, such as the Madonna,
the Mona Lisa, or an ermine. If you do not have access
to a reproduction, write a poem based on a favorite
piece of art.

APRIL

16

. . . .

Return Of The Extinct Animal

Write a poem about an extinct animal coming back to life in the present day. Examples: plesiosaur, saber-toothed tiger, Carolina parakeet. Describe its physical features, habitat requirements, and other interesting facts. Feel free to invent information and/or have your animal talk, time-travel, possess telekinetic powers, fly, etc.

APRIL

17

. . . .

He Said / She Said

Write a poem in two voices. Instead of using quotation marks and "he said/she said" conventions, use stanza breaks to distinguish who's speaking. Suggestions for pair-ups: Cleopatra and Margaret Thatcher; Thoreau and Emerson; Emily Dickinson and Prince; two sides of yourself.

APRIL

18

· ·

Father Of The Beats

Today is the birthday of Bob Kaufman, founding father of the Beat Generation of poets. In honor of Kaufman's contribution to American letters, write a poem that relies on spontaneous invention, vibrant sonics, and the tones and structures of jazz. To get in a bebop frame of mind read a selection of Kaufman's poems at the Modern American Poetry website: http://www.english.illinois.edu/maps/poets/g_l/kaufman/kaufman.htm If you do not have access to the Internet, write a poem that begins with the line *I have folded my sorrows into the mantle of summer night,* from Kaufman's poem, "I have folded my sorrows."

APRIL

19

. . . .

Death Bed

Suppose you live to a ripe old age and die of old age. Describe your thoughts and activities during your final day. What achievements are you happy/proud about? What are your regrets? Be specific. You might be proud of the fact that you braved the "Bucket Drop" at White Water Water Park, but regret you didn't sample the funnel cake. Have your poem end with your final breath/thought.

APRIL

20

. . . .

Mother Tongue

The poet Adrienne Rich summed it up completely with
this title from her 1993 collection: *Your Native
Land/Your Life*. Write a poem that borrows language
from your mother tongue, which could also be your
father tongue. Consider using some of the phrases or
sayings you heard in the household during your
childhood. For added inspiration, read Eduardo C.
Corral's "In Colorado My Father Scoured and Stacked
Dishes" available at:

http://www.poetryfoundation.org/poetrymagazin
e/poem/243752

APRIL

21

. . . .

Your Favorite Word/s

On this date in 1828, Noah Webster published the first American dictionary. In honor of this great accomplishment visit the Merriam-Webster website at: http://www.merriam-webster.com/ and type some of your favorite words into the search box. You can also use the dictionary from your bookshelf and look up your favorite words. Now, write a poem that defines a word or words by providing sample usages, synonyms, antonyms, and a word or words it rhymes with. If you do not have access to the Internet or a dictionary, consider writing a poem using some of the definitions of the word *hack*: to cut or sever, to annoy or vex, to clear, to loaf, to cope, to cough, board on which a hawk is fed, a prison guard, to drive a cab, to ride a horse, cliché, stale, threadbare.

APRIL

22

. . . .

Earth Day

On this date in 1970, Earth Day was celebrated for the first time. In honor of this day, take a moment to read Wendell Berry's poem "The Peace of Wild Things" at: http://www.poetryfoundation.org/poem/171140.
In this poem, Berry becomes peaceful and free in the presence of wood drakes and herons. In your poem, share what you do when overwhelmed by environmental degradation, where you go and what appeases you when pollution and carbon emissions drive you to despair. Include specific images in your poem about the place you have chosen to retreat.

APRIL

23

. . . .

Shakespearean Sonnet

In honor of Shakespeare's birthday, write a Shakespearean sonnet (14 lines of iambic pentameter with the rhyme scheme ABAB/CDCD/EFEF/GG) on the subject of love. To bring your sonnet up to date, allude to at least four pop songs with the word *love* in the title. Examples: "I Think I Love You," "Baby Love," "What's Love Got to Do With It," "Tainted Love."

APRIL

24

. . . .

No Ideas But In Things

In honor of George Oppen's birthday (b. 1908), write a poem in the style of the objectivists, looking clearly and closely at the world and presenting images without interpretation/explanation or personal bias. As you write and revise, be sincere and intelligent, viewing your poem as you would an object. Examples: a discarded supermarket cart in a ditch; balls of cottonwood fluff clinging to cobwebs. For more inspiration, read a sampling of Oppen's poems at:

www.poets.org/poet.php/prmPID/920.

APRIL

25

. . . .

So This Is _____

In honor of Ted Kooser's birthday on this date in 1939, read or listen to his poem "So This Is Nebraska" www.poetryfoundation.org/poem/171336 published in his collection *Sure Signs*, then write a poem that models the title. Whether or not you read his poem, your poem for today should begin by describing a landscape as you drive/float/walk by it. Use extended metaphor to describe the structures, scenery, and animals/people you pass. Toward the end of your poem, address yourself in the second person: What do you feel like doing? What do you do instead?

APRIL

26

. . . .

A Horse Walks Into A Bar

All humans are hardwired for humor. A sense of humor
may have provided an evolutionary advantage as a way
of diffusing tension/conflict between and among
clans/tribes. Psychologists posit that in telling or
laughing at a joke, we signal to others our values and
beliefs. Write a poem that explores the role of humor in
human culture. For extra credit, add in names of your
favorite comedians or one-liners from their skits.

APRIL

27

. . . .

Elegy

Write an elegy for a specific time in your life that you miss (high school, college, a time you lived in a different city or country, etc.). Include in your elegy poem the words *forget, secret, scatter, dusk,* and *bereft.*

APRIL

28

. . . .

The Edible School Yard

In honor of the renowned chef and food activist Alice Waters, write a poem titled "The Edible School Yard." While you might decide to conduct research about this Berkeley endeavor to bring "real" food to school-aged children, you are also free to let your imagination move in directions not based on actual events regarding the School Lunch Initiative, such as the imagined day when pizza and burgers are no longer served in public schools.

APRIL

29

• •

Beautiful And Dangerous

In honor of Yusef Kumunyakaa's birthday (b. 1947), write a poem inspired by his poem "Slam, Dunk, and Hook," about an activity (playing baseball, doing gymnastics, skimboarding, skiing, etc.) wherein the speaker feels both beautiful and dangerous. Kumunyakaa writes: *We outmaneuvered the footwork / of bad angels* and of being *poised in midair / like storybook sea monsters.* To read his entire poem, check out his collection *Pleasure Dome: New & Selected Poems*, or find it online at:

http://www.aaregistry.org/poetry/view/slam-dunk-hook-yusef-komunyakaa

APRIL

30

. . . .

What's In A Name?

Everyone's given name has a story behind it. What's the story behind yours? Perhaps you are named after a saint, a Biblical character, or your great-grandmother. Brainstorm a list of everything you can recall about the meaning and derivation of your name. You may share what your name literally means or how it reveals your cultural heritage. The meat of this exercise is to go deep—sharing, as poet Marilyn Chin does, much maligned Asian-American stereotypes. You might have almost been named something else. Share that story. Or write about what might have happened if you had a different name. If you are cloudy on the details about how you got your name (or its history), make them up. For extra inspiration, check out Marilyn Chin's "How I Got that Name" at:

www.poets.org/viewmedia.php/prmMID/15631

MAY

1

· ·

May Day

Look up the names of flowers that grow in your geographical location and write a poem using at least ten of those names in a poem. Also, feel free to use the names of flowers in unusual ways, such as *I slipped on my ladyslippers* or *she hollyhocked her way into our conversation.*

2

. . . .

Weather Or Not

On this day in 1982, the Weather Channel premiered on cable television. Write a poem that isn't about the weather, but weaves your local weather forecast throughout it, allowing the forecast to reflect the tone of the poem. If the poem is about a broken relationship, consider mentioning lightning and thunder. If it is about a honeymoon, you might describe a clear, crisp night. End the poem with an image that reveals a drastic change in the weather. Feel free to use the vocabulary of meteorologists including, but not limited to phrases like *storm surge, a cold front moving in, hurricane watch,* or *another day of rain.*

3

. . . .

Mysterious Life Of Washington, D.C.

On this day in 1802, Washington D.C. was incorporated. There have been many myths and legends about Washington D.C., from why there is no J Street to the Hope Diamond being cursed. Research and find a favorite Washington D.C. myth or legend to write about, or make up a myth or legend of your own about the city and see what new tale you can create.

MAY

4

. . . .

Breaking The Rules

Make a list of all the "rules" you've been taught about writing poetry such as "show, don't tell," "never use the word *soul* in a poem," "never end a line on the word *the,*" "never write in lowercase," or "never leave a poem untitled." Come up with a list of rules you've either made for yourself or someone's told you. Now, write a poem that breaks at least four of these rules. Extra credit: write a poem that breaks all the rules.

5

Pat, I'd Like To Buy A Vowel

Make a list of twelve words that have the same vowel sounds (*bee, treat, pepperoni, eagle*) and use five to ten of them repetitively throughout a poem. Extra credit: write a poem for each of the vowel sounds.

6

. . . .

Large Subject, Small Poem

Make a list of five of the largest things you can think of, such as an elephant, a skyscraper, a planet, or the universe. Your list may also include large abstractions, such as an ego or appetite. Now write a poem of four lines or less about this big subject.

MAY

7

. . . .

Around The Corner Comes
Dumb Luck

On this day in 1977, Seattle Slew won the Kentucky Derby. Since racehorses have the most interesting names, look up the names of horses (they don't have to be famous) and use ten to fifteen of them in a poem. Or make a list of your own made-up humorous, poignant, or whimsical racehorse names. Write a poem about something other than a horse race using either list of names.

MAY

8

· ·

Paper Or Laptop?

For this exercise, if you normally write your poem on paper, write it on a computer. If you normally start your poem on a laptop, use a journal or write it out long hand. Write about feeling cold, either emotionally or physically; and next, write another poem about being warm the way you normally write. Extra credit: if writing longhand, write with your non-dominate hand and see how this changes the poem.

MAY

9

. . . .

Metaphor Metaphor

Think about something that is or was a challenge for you—it can be anything from learning how to waterski to remembering where you put your keys. Write twenty metaphors about the topic you chose. For example, if you chose misplacing your keys, you could write, "my keys are a buried treasure" or "my keys are fog, in front of me then gone." Allow yourself to have some fun, seeing if you can stretch your metaphor—"my keys are Elvis and have left the building, my keys are songsung blue." Keep pushing yourself to make your metaphors more wild and strange. When you have your list of twenty metaphors, write a poem using your favorites from the bunch.

MAY

10

. . . .

Feels Like The First Time

On this date in 1994, Nelson Mandela became the first black president of South Africa. Write a poem that explores the first of something. It can be a political or historical event, or a personal first, like the first time you ate Key lime pie or gave or received a bouquet of flowers. Make a list of twenty "firsts" to see what topic inspires you, then write a poem about one or several of these "firsts."

11

. . . .

Psychic Poet

Write a poem where you pretend you can see into the future. It can be serious, funny, dark, or light in tone. Who's president in 2032? What does communicating look like? What are people wearing? What color is the sky? What does the ocean taste like? Allow yourself to play with your future scenario and be specific and detailed. Do you need a crystal ball to see the future? Tea leaves?

MAY

12

· ·

Back From The Past

Write a poem where a famous person from the past visits you in the present. What message does s/he bring to you? What does s/he want to tell you? Write a series of questions for this person and imagine the person answering them. Write down everything s/he says. Use the best answers and lines from this exercise to write a poem about a topic this person brings to mind. After you complete your draft, research this person and find an actual quote to use as an epigraph or weave into the poem.

MAY

13

· ·

Classical Jazz

Sit in a comfy chair (with or without a glass of wine) and listen to jazz or classical music for fifteen to twenty minutes. Have a notebook to jot down images or ideas that come to mind as you listen to the music. Write a poem about something you thought of while you listened. If you like, keep the music on while you write.

14

· ·

Father Figure

Write a poem about your father or a father figure in
your life. In the poem, mention the type of shoes he
wore, what he ate for breakfast, and reference at least
three fathers from television shows. Write to find out
where these three images will lead you and what story
your poem wants to tell.

15

· ·

Emily Lives

On this day in 1886, Emily Dickinson died at the age of fifty-five. Imagine Emily Dickinson sitting next to you right now, dressed in white, and holding a book of poems. She reads quietly by your side. Write a poem about this scene or imagine you are writing a letter to Emily Dickinson. What do you want to tell her?

16

. . . .

The "You" Poem

Think about all the people in your life that you liked, but never really got a chance to know. This could be because they died or perhaps you just had a brief friendship before you had to move away. Maybe you switched jobs or your relationship was cut short for another reason. Write a poem where you address this person. Share with her/him images of your favorite things and things s/he never knew that were important to you. Be specific. If you love flatbread from Spain or love dinner-plate dahlias, mention it. Tell them what you remember of them. You can write this poem in the form of a letter, postcard, or just address the poem to them: *Dear _____, You never saw my garden...*

17

. . . .

Index Card Fun

Find an index card and turn it vertically. Write a poem about something that doesn't last long. Writing on an index card vertically will result in much shorter lines— see how this added structure changes how you normally write. For extra credit, turn the index card over and write horizontally about something that lasts a long time.

18

I Don't Know Where I'm Gonna Go When The Volcano Blows

On this day in 1980, Washington State's Mount St. Helens erupted, sending ash in the air for miles. Write a poem that compares a relationship, person, lover, family, job, or divorce to a volcano. Learn about the differences in volcanoes, such as the slow moving lava of Hawaiian volcanoes to the almost atomic-blast ash clouds of Mount St. Helens.

19

. . . .

A Pair Of Couplets

Write a poem about a pair of something (or a pair of people) in couplet form (a couplet is a two-line stanza). Make sure each line in the couplet complements the other in sound and image; for example, if your first line is about a bride maybe include an image of a groom in the second line or perhaps a veil or bouquet. Make a list of pairs—*Bert and Ernie, apples and oranges, his and hers*—then write a poem in couplets inspired by the couple you choose.

20

· ·

Rosanna Rosanna Danna

On this day in 1989, comedian and *Saturday Night Live* cast member, Gilda Radner died of cancer. While on *Saturday Night Live*, Gilda played a recurring character named Rosanna Rosanna Danna who went on long rants about something she had misheard, such as "I don't understand why people say there's too much *violins* on TV" (instead of violence). At the end of her rant, she would say "Never mind." Think about words or phrases you've misheard or words and phrases that sound like different things, for example, "Les Miserables" sounds like "Lame is Rob" or "sugar" sounds like "Should ya?" Write a poem that uses some misheard lines, either with or without the speaker realizing s/he has heard them incorrectly.

21

. . . .

Langston's Titles

Choose eight or more of these titles from Langston Hughes' poems—"Acceptance," "April Rain Song," "Bad Morning," "Bouquet," "Cultural Exchange," "Daybreak in Alabama," "Dream Variations," "Genius Child," "Juke Box Love Song," "Life is Fine," "Night Funeral in Harlem," "Quiet Girl," "Sea Calm," "Snake," "The Weary Blues," "When Sue Wears Red"—and weave then into a poem about something beautiful or something you wish would happen.

22

. . . .

Mysteries Inside

The author of *The Adventures of Sherlock Holmes*, Sir Arthur Conan Doyle, was born today. Write a poem infused with mystery. In your poem, explore a big mystery, such as the Bermuda Triangle, whether aliens exist, or whether Elvis is still alive, or have the word "mystery" hidden somewhere in it. Maybe it starts with a question it never answers. Whether you define "mystery" as something you don't know the answer to or as the van from *Scooby-Doo,* your goal for today is to get mysterious.

23

....

Library Field Trip

On this day in 1911, President Taft dedicated the New York Public Library. For today's poem, take a trip to your local library, taking notes on what you see, hear, smell, and touch. Think about how libraries have changed from housing those wonderful wooden card catalogues to computer checkout systems. Take notes about the experience—the scents, sounds, and colors, how the books feel or the carpet sounds as you walk across it. Be specific. Write a poem that takes place in a library using as much detail as possible. Or write a poem about being locked in a library overnight or falling in love with another library patron or the librarian.

24

....

What's In The Pantry?

Walk into your pantry or open your cupboard and choose three, boxed food items, such as cake mix, lemon bars, tabouli mix, cereal, instant pudding, or even dog bones. Once you have your three boxes, read over all the information written on each side of the box. As you do this, take notes on interesting phrasing or what surprises or inspires you. Maybe it's the recipe for "Amazing Cheesecake Lemon Bars" or maybe on your gingerbread cake mix there's information on how "intricately decorated gingerbread cakes were given by fair ladies to knights." Use whatever information you find, including the ingredients. Now write a poem that uses images, words, and phrases from your boxed foods. Have the poem be about something other than the three items you chose.

MAY

25

. . . .

Taboo You

Write a poem that you would be afraid to show someone because of what it might reveal about you or someone else. Allow yourself to write about something you aren't 100% comfortable with others knowing about you or your family. Write a poem that makes you feel a little vulnerable; this can be from having certain words in your poem that you have never used or a subject you find taboo. Allow yourself the opportunity to write this poem, remembering it is your choice whether you want to share it with anyone.

26

A-Z

Write a poem where the first word starts with "A" and the last word of the poem ends with "Z." Somewhere in the poem mention the alphabet or alphabetical order. Have the poem be about something that has nothing to do with the alphabet. For extra credit, try to use a word that begins with each letter of the alphabet.

27

. . . .

Contrary Day

Write a poem in a way you don't normally write. If you usually write short poems, write a long poem. If you often write narrative poems, write a poem that's more experimental and abstract. If you find yourself ready to use a technique or word you normally use, use something completely different. Have the poem be about something you rarely write about. See what happens when you write differently.

28

. . . .

Bridging The Gap

On this day in 1937, the Golden Gate Bridge officially opened. To give a nod to this fact, write a poem that bridges the gap between two topics. Choose two subjects that have nothing to do with each other, and write a poem that includes both subjects and creates a bridge between them. You can write about peacocks and caramel apples, movie stars and typewriters. Choose two subjects that seem to have nothing in common, but find a way to make them connect.

29

. . . .

Hope, Thanks, And Memories

On this day in 1903, comedian Bob Hope was born. Bob Hope was known for his own rendition of the song "Thanks For The Memories." Write a poem where you give thanks, but make sure it includes humor as well as gratitude.

30

. . . .

Mixed Travel Plans

Write two ten-line poems about two places you've visited—one that you loved and one you disliked or didn't like as well. Now, intersperse the lines of the place-you-loved poem with the lines of the place-you-didn't-like-so-much poem until you have one twenty-line poem.

31

Big Ben

On this day in 1859, Big Ben became a working clock in London, England. For a long time, hearing the bells throughout the city was how Londoners knew what time it was. Write a poem where the reader knows what time it is and what season it is through the details of your poem. Do not use words like *morning, evening, winter, summer,* but let the poem reflect the time of day or season by what is happening in the poem and by the images you use. For extra credit, have someone in the poem running late or showing up early.

JUNE

1

. . . .

Lovely Rita Meter Maid

On this date in 1967, the Beatles released *Sgt. Pepper's Lonely Hearts Club Band*, which sold over eight million copies worldwide. For today, write a poem that mimics the metrical beats or the general phrasing of "Fixing a Hole," "She's Leaving Home," "Good Morning" or another song from this iconic band.

2

. . . .

Curse

Write a poem that begins by taking aim at a grievance
or hatred but ends with coming to terms with that
grievance. You may rant against polluters, climate
change skeptics, text messaging addicts, or anything else
that's bothering you. In Miroslav Holub's poem "Man
Cursing the Sea," the speaker reels against the sea,
calling it a *pettifogging pawnbroker of shells* and a *slow, slimy
copy of the sky.* Aim to infuse your invective with the
similar deft sound orchestration, such as assonance and
alliteration.

3

. . . .

Country Of Origin

In celebration of poet Allen Ginsberg, who was born on this day in 1926, write a poem that, as Ginsberg does in his poem "America," addresses the country you were born and/or raised in. Ginsberg states *America, I've given you my all and now I am nothing... America, when will we end the human war? America, go fuck yourself with your atom bomb.* In your poem, repeat the name of your country at the beginning of most lines. Make sure to include specifics about what your birth country has and hasn't done for you. You can read or listen to Allen Ginsberg at:

http://www.poetryarchive.org/poetryarchive/singlePoem.do?poemId=1548

4

· ·

The Right To Vote

On June 4, 1919, Congress, by joint resolution, approved the women's suffrage amendment. At long last, women in America had the right to vote. Commemorate this important date by writing a poem about what it would take for you to be truly free, reflecting on what keeps you or others oppressed. American poet William Stafford states that freedom is not following a river or following a river—it depends on which you want. To get started, use the incantation *I am waiting...* to share what you are waiting for. For added inspiration, see Lawrence Ferlinghetti's poem "I Am Waiting" at:

www.poetryfoundation.org/poem/171598.

JUNE

5

· ·

Field Guide To The Animals

In celebration of nature-loving poet David Wagoner's birthday, take yourself and your notebook to a beach, wooded park, or zoo; anywhere you can observe the natural world. Once you get there, find an animal and pay close attention to what it is doing and what it looks like. Jot down notes as you watch your chosen critter, then go home and turn these observations into a poem, daring yourself to find offbeat and quirky ways to describe your chosen animal. For example, D.H. Lawrence's "Snake" states: *He lifted his head from his drinking as cattle do, / And looked at me vaguely, as drinking cattle do.* Wagoner's poem "Peacock Display" is another fine example:

www.poetryfoundation.org/poem/171094.

JUNE

6

. . . .

D-Day

June 6 is the anniversary of D-Day, the invasion of
Normandy by 160,000 ground troops, 197,000 naval
personnel, 12,000 planes, and 7,000 vessels. To keep
the Germans from finding out about this invasion,
allied forces concocted Operation Fortitude, a fake plan
to invade Norway. They constructed dummy camps
using scaffolding and canvas, brought in inflatable
trucks and tanks, and broadcast white noise over Axis-
accessible radio waves, which the Germans expended
much effort attempting to decode. Write a persona
poem in the voice of a soldier involved in Operation
Fortitude. Your soldier might initially mask his fears
with bravado and machismo, alluding to the many
devices created to dupe the Germans, but by the end of
the poem, he may reach a state of humble acceptance.

7

· ·

Who Are You?

Nikki Giovanni, whose birthday is today, states in her poem "Cotton Candy on a Rainy Day":

It seems no matter how I try I become more difficult
        to hold
I am not an easy woman
to want

Write a poem that defines who you are: are you becoming more difficult to hold? Are you an easy woman/man or a difficult one? Share details about yourself using concrete imagery and forthright language in an open/free-verse poem that describes and defines you.

8

. . . .

Decade, Decade On The Wall

Choose a decade and write a poem about that era, evoking that specific time period's fashions, hairstyles, slang, dance crazes, etc. For inspiration, read Rose Kelleher's "Free Bird," excerpted here:

Let sideburns reign; let white guys wear cologne;
let jeans reveal who's well and fully grown
from groin to groove—it's like a manhood-fest.

9

. . . .

Rock Star

On this date in 1972, Bruce Springsteen signed his first big record deal with Columbia Records. Write a poem about a favorite lyricist, musician, or band. Make sure to pay homage to your rock icon with vivid imagery. Make it clear why your chosen musician is worthy of tribute in a poem. To get inspired, here's the beginning of "Ray Charles On Late Night TV" by David Graham:

That nonstop rhinestone grin
undimmed by the decades,
though the hair is frosty gray
and the face a bit grizzled—

he whips out the intro
to What'd I Say, as
the latest Raeletts
sway against their tambourines...

10

. . . .

Spam It Up

Head to your email SPAM folder, and write a poem that incorporates the poorly translated ads for black market Viagra and other stamina enhancers. Examples: "Virility paradise is here," "Great cucumber is your wealth," "Subject her to a punishing ride," and "This has the potential to completely ruin you." Write your poem from the point of view of the spammer who claims to have a "Strange trick to make girls moan!" Alternatively, write a narrative poem in the voice of someone who actually talks this way.

JUNE

11

. . . .

Found

For this poem, head to a used bookstore or library and find a book to steal a poem from. How-to manuals and obscure reference books are good possibilities to investigate. Another sure bet is pet-care guides: *Know Your Budgie* or *How to Clip a Poodle*. Another option, if you are far from a library or bookstore, is to borrow from instruction manuals, street signs, emergency procedure bulletins, etc. Officially, a found poem author can remove words from a text, but none may be added. Also, the line sequence cannot be altered. If you are looking for more examples, Annie Dillard's *Mornings Like This* is an entire book of found poems. Definitions and more examples may be found at:

http://www.poets.org/viewmedia.php/prmMID/5780

JUNE

12

. . . .

Statue Of Elvis Found On Mars

Pick up a copy of Sun or The National Enquirer. Scan the headlines and choose an article that peeks your poetry brain or choose from one of the following:

Moth Baby Eats Mattress
500 Foot Jesus Appears at UN
Doctors Reveal: How You Steam Your Rice Says Something About You!
I Was Bigfoot's Love Slave
Saddam And Osama Adopt Shaved Ape Baby

In your poem, make up details about your chosen headline. What did Jesus tell folks when he showed up at the UN? Perhaps he had a message about world peace or where to purchase the best matzo. What was it like to be Bigfoot's love slave—grueling job, I bet.

JUNE

13

. . . .

Inaugural Poem

If you were chosen as the inaugural poet for the next incoming American president, what would you write about? Elizabeth Alexander included the stitching of hems, darning and patching, *repairing things in need of repair.* Richard Blanco shared about *pencil-yellow school buses* and fruit stands *arrayed like rainbows.* If given the chance, what words would you choose to welcome a new leader? In Maya Angelou's poem, a rock cries out, while Miller Williams' focus is on children and the *disenfranchised dead.* Will you ask questions? Will you provide answers? It's entirely up to you.

JUNE

14

. . . .

Flag Day

In honor of Flag Day, write a poem addressed to the
American Flag. It might be an inexpensive flag on a
stick, a flag to be draped on a veteran's casket, or Jasper
Johns' painting, *Flag*. Maybe you want to thank it, or
scorn it, or some of each. What do its colors remind
you of? Try to be objective about its configuration of
stars and stripes. What feelings does it evoke? Whitman
describes it as "teeming with life" and a "death flag."
Don't be afraid to contradict yourself as you view this
symbol of America as both constructive and
destructive. For more inspiration, read Walt Whitman's
poem "Delicate Cluster":

http://www.poets.org/viewmedia.php/prmMID/
20737

JUNE

15

. . . .

Talking Visual Art

Mona Lisa, Frida Kahlo, Gaughin's Tahitian beauties, Picasso's *Demoiselle's d'Avignon*: for the poem you write for today, someone or something in a painting or sculpture will be the speaker. If you have Internet access, peruse the Metropolitan Museum (http://www.metmuseum.org) or Museum of Modern Art (http://www.moma.org) websites. If not, rely on your memory or a reproduction in your possession. To avoid clichés and obvious declarations, have the speaker be an inanimate object or group of objects, such as each of the pastries in Claes Oldenburg's *Pastry Case, I*.

JUNE

16

. . . .

The Good, The Bad, And The Ugly

Choose a political leader, celebrity, or other celebrated figure, sharing that person's strengths and weaknesses. For instance, Thomas Jefferson purchased the Louisiana Territory and allowed the Alien and Sedition Acts to end, but kept a slave as his concubine. Write a poem that praises as well as indicts.

JUNE

17

· ·

American Sentences

Allen Ginsberg is the brainchild of these seventeen-syllable length sentences, a quasi-precursor to Twitterature. American Sentences are haiku-like in their heavy reliance on image and the tension created in the two-parted structure. Example: The Sign at Dairy Queen Reads: *New Flame Thrower Chicken Now Hiring*. Write a poem consisting of seventeen-syllable sentences on any topic.

18

. . . .

Experiments With Reading

Spend some time reading from three very different texts. Examples: *The Bible, Chainsaw Savvy*, and a guide to birds. Your poem for today will find a way to include information, images, or insights from all three of these sources because, as Robert Pinsky once said, "When writing a poem, incongruities are your friend."

19

. . . .

Scaffolding

Choose a favorite poem you've written, and write down at least six of your favorite lines from that poem. Now spend five or ten minutes freewriting right below each of these lines. Take what you've written and shape it into a poem. You may or may not decide to remove the borrowed lines.

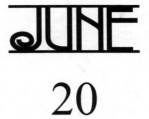

20

. . . .

Giving Back

In celebration of Paul Muldoon's birthday, today's exercise is based on one of his poems titled "Extraordinary Rendition." In it the poet creates a two-part structure, one half detailing "What I Gave You Back" and the other offering up "What You Gave Me Back." Write a poem where you do one action in the first section of your poem, and the opposite in the second part to create your own divvying-up poem. You can read "Extraordinary Rendition" here:

www.poets.org/viewmedia.php/prmMID/21847

21

. . . .

Solstice

In celebration of the longest day of the year, write a poem that incorporates five of the following words: *luminous, bedazzling, sunny, saturated, radiant, incandescent, illustrious, bright.* Afterwards, go outside and see if you can soak up a little Vitamin D and read your poem to the native birds.

JUNE

22

. . . .

Year Of Your Birth

What historic events occurred during the year you were born? What was invented? What wars began or ended? Gather up significant events and shape them into a poem. Use the first line of Sandra McPherson's "1943," *I was born the year of____* as a jumping off place. Her poem begins *I was born the year of the grey pennies,* but you might have been born the year birth control pills first went on the market. Share interesting and quirky details about the year of your birth. For added inspiration, listen to Charles Simic reading his poem, "1938": http://www.youtube.com/watch?v=aU2Wp0PaTx 8

JUNE

23

. . . .

Self-Taught

Anna Akhmatova, whose birthday is today, wrote a poem titled "I Taught Myself to Live Simply and Wisely." Maybe you've learned how to live extravagantly, or within your means, or stupidly. Write either a serious or comic poem about what you've taught yourself.

JUNE

24

. . . .

Opposites

Create a two-column list of twenty personality characteristics (it may or may not be you). Examples: *night owl, gregarious, extrovert, adventurous*. Next, create a second list alongside it with the exact opposite characteristics: *early bird, quiet, introvert, careful*. Using your two lists, write a poem in two voices, alternating between each list. For instance, have the night owl address the early bird while sharing breakfast, or have the socialite and hermit show up together at a party. Alternatively, list ten adjectives to describe yourself, then write a poem in the voice of your opposite.

JUNE

25

. . . .

One Degree Of Separation

Do you have a friend who is friends with someone famous? Or knows someone who shook the hand of JKF? In 1954, my father gave William Faulkner a lift to his classroom at the University of Virginia. Write a narrative poem that tells about a time either you or someone you know had a brush with someone famous.

JUNE

26

· ·

The Story Of Words

Tell the story of how you learned a particular word or words. Examples: I learned "omit" in 1970 from my grandfather's obituary, which stated "Omit flowers." I learned the word "impeach" while playing the dictionary game in 1974. A few weeks later, the Watergate saga began to unfold, and I knew all about impeachment thanks to our game of randomly looking up words and positing definitions. Your poem will not only provide information on when/where you learned a new word, but will aim for a dance between the ethereal quality of memory and the concrete nature of words.

JUNE

27

· ·

Blessing

In celebration of Lucille Clifton's birthday, write a poem of blessing modeled after Clifton's poem "blessing the boats":

www.poets.org/viewmedia.php/prmMID/16489

Your poem should have at least three clauses that begin with directives starting with *may*… and it should also use elements of nature (water, wind, tide) to make abstract nouns more concrete (fear, love, innocence).

28

· ·

Road Trip

For this poem, take a drive down a specific road, turnpike, throughway, or highway. Stop at a café or restaurant and take notes about what you see, the conversations you overhear, the bumper stickers and the logos on semis and mobile homes. Fashion a poem from your road trip notes.

JUNE

29

. . . .

Hate

What do you hate? I'm not particularly fond of guavas, synthetic fabrics, or costume jewelry. Fashion a poem from your list of things you'd rather not eat, drink, wear, hear, or see. For more inspiration, do a quick Internet search to find Charles Simic's poem "Our Salvation" to get your invective juices flowing.

JUNE

30

. . . .

What Will You Tell The Aliens

Your writing task for today is to encapsulate what it is to be human into a poem of ten lines or less that pivots on two central images that sum up the human condition. Perhaps your two images are a football and a grassy field or a wedding feast and a funeral parlor. If you need to see an example of this exercise in action, have a gander at Jean Follain's "Signs for Travelers," which appears in his book *Transparence of the World*, translated by W.S. Merwin, which can be found online through an Internet search.

JULY

JULY

1

. . . .

Poem of Place

We're exactly halfway through the calendar year. Spend two minutes freewriting a list of places you'd like to visit during the second half of the year—a trout-stocked mountain lake, a local art museum, a faraway country such as India. Choose one destination from your list and, after doing a little research, write a poem about that place.

JULY

2

· ·

Apology

Happy birthday to Nobel Prize-winning poet Wislawa Szymborska! Szymborska, born in Western Poland and a lifelong resident of Krakow, was known not only for her fiercely political poems but for revealing the profound truths in the everyday experience of living. In her honor, today's assignment is to write a poem of apology. Don't apologize for minor things, like forgetting to close the windows during a rainstorm; apologize to abstractions such as hope, necessity, chance, and loyalty. For further inspiration, read Szymborska's poem "Under a Certain Little Star," which can be found through an Internet search.

JULY

3

. . . .

What's Your Cultural Identity?

When we're asked to write about our cultural or ethnic heritage, we often clam up or lapse into cliché. Two remedies against this: (1) write a poem in a form with a tight rhyme scheme; and (2) instead of focusing directly on your cultural identity, share who you are by describing a beloved possession and your relation to it. For an example, check out Erica Dawson's "High Heel," from her book *Big-Eyed Afraid* online at *The Barefoot Muse:*

http://www.everseradio.com/high-heel-by-erica-dawson-in-the-best-of-the-barefoot-muse

4

. . . .

Fourth Of July

If you live in the U.S., you may be knocked back into your childhood as each bottle rocket and Roman candle squeals and crackles throughout the day. What do you remember about the 4th of July celebrations of your childhood? I recall how my mother served up sandwich meats, Kaiser rolls, pickles, and coleslaw on red, white and blue plates. Uncle Matt set a bush on fire in the yard, and we almost had to call the fire department to put it out. Write a poem that shares Independence Day memories.

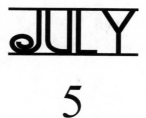

JULY

5

· ·

Don Your Dali Moustache Day

It's the birthday of Jean Couteau, surrealist poet and playwright. In honor of his birthday, write a surrealist poem today. One way to do this is to begin with a 5-minute automatic writing session. Write as fast as you can without thinking logically or worrying about making sense. When you are finished with your timed writing, read it over and highlight passages that interest you. Using these passages as triggers, continue writing fast. Once you've done this, shape this raw and strange material into a poem.

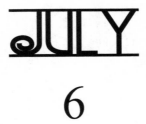

6

. . . .

Winter In July

Open up a box of stored holiday decorations or visit a
holiday website (Oriental Trading has an extensive
online catalog), and study the nativity tablecloths,
candles, snowman mugs, and menorahs. If you don't
want to think about the holidays in July, open a catch-
all drawer and take out a few odd items. Write a poem
in the voice of a future anthropologist attempting to
make sense of these "artifacts."

7

· ·

How To Cook A Wolf

On this date in 1908, food writer MFK Fisher was born. In honor of her birthday, write a poem in which a specific food or foods, or a recipe, figures. Scan a cookbook and make a list of verbs that have to do with cooking/baking: *truss, whip, broil, braise, beat.* Aim to include some of these verbs in your poem.

8

. . . .

Good Humor Ice Cream Truck

Freewrite on this topic for five minutes. In your freewrite, try to describe your childhood memories of summer evenings using all five of your senses. What did the cooling asphalt smell like? How did it feel on your tongue to lick the wooden Strawberry Shortcake stick? Write a poem that allows the reader to experience your youthful memories.

9

Phobias

This exercise is inspired by the poetry of Aimee Nezhukumatathil, author of *At the Drive-in Volcano* (Tupelo Press, 2007). Write a poem about one or more phobias. Do you have alliumphobia, a fear of garlic? Or how about enetophobia, a fear of pins? You can access a complete list of phobias at:

www.phobialist.com.

For inspiration, take a peek at Aimee's wonderful poem, "Hippopotomonstrosesquippedaliophobia," published at:

www.slate.com/articles/arts/poem/2004/01/hipp opotomonstrosesquippedaliophobia.html

JULY

10

. . . .

Search-Engines

Google, Bing, Altavista, HotBot, Excite: pick a search engine and type two very unrelated words in the search box: *telescope dog, carpet melody, pie astronomy, lemon string.* Write a poem based on what businesses, articles, and blog posts contain both of your words. If you're without an Internet connection, walk around your surroundings putting two objects together to create these paired words, such as: *salt-shaker hat, penny cat, teacup basket.* Write a poem using these unique word combinations.

JULY

11

· ·

She Blinded Me With Science

Pick up a copy of *Science, Nature,* or another science magazine, or log onto the *New York Times'* Science Times (http://www.nytimes.com/pages/science), and peruse articles about the biochemistry of skin tissue, the fossil record of prehistoric gnawing, and caterpillars that display false eye and face patterns. Write a poem that incorporates some of the wonders of the natural world.

JULY

12

. . . .

Channeling Neruda's Wildness

On this day in 1904, Pablo Neruda was born. One of the 20th century's greatest and most influential poets, Neruda self-published his first book, *Crepusculario*. In honor of his birthday, channel Neruda's untamed wildness with regard to metaphor, writing a poem that takes risks with language. For example, instead of relying on clichés when describing clouds (*soft white pillows*) or rain (*it was coming down like cats and dogs*), compare a cloud to a giant feather boa, or the rain to a pack of wild horses falling from the sky.

JULY

13

· ·

Burden Basket

For today's poem, begin by making a list of your burdens. They may be real or imagined, great or small, but make sure they are specific; for instance, not "my child," but "the weekly trips to the sensory gym and speech therapy." Once you've done this, make an accompanying list of your pleasures: knitting, berry picking, fishing, calligraphy. Write a poem that contrasts your passions with your commitments using "because" to create anaphora, the literary term for the repetition of a word or phrase at the beginning of successive clauses. Example: *Because I rehabilitate in a stuffy gym each Tuesday afternoon, I fill my basket with blueberries, my ego dissolving with each plunk. Because I writhe at the suggestion that I must break into a sweat, I recline in my chaise, blueberries unbrooding my brain.*

14

. . . .

Burrowing

Today we're going to burrow like crabs. To start
digging, set a timer for six minutes and freewrite off a
randomly-chosen line or phrase. Examples: *the donut hole
is thriving* or *a cloud stretching a thousand miles.* When the
chimer chimes, reset it for four minutes and make the
last three words you've written the first three words of
your next freewrite. Repeat this process two more times
(setting the timer for six and then four minutes). This
slight pause and backing up will allow you to go deeper.
Later, extract the best parts of this exercise and turn it
into a poem.

15

. . . .

One-Rhyme Poem

Write a poem in which each line ends with the same rhyme. The easiest rhyme to use is the "er" sound, as in *peanut-butter, lecher, muster, jester, lover, cracker, beggar.* For an excellent example of the one-rhyme form, see David Wagoner's "Junior High School Band Concert":
http://www.poets.org/viewmedia.php/prmMID/15383

16

. . . .

What's Funny About A Headstone

Write a comic poem (it may or may not turn serious) about choosing your own or someone else's grave marker. Situate yourself at a monument store, observing the many sizes, shapes, and designs. Will you choose a headstone festooned with stars and lilies or a plain block of granite? What will be your epitaph? Where would you like to be buried? Consider sharing details about who will visit your grave and what they might feel or say.

JULY

17

· ·

Meeting The Parents

Write a poem in the voice of your mother or father (biological, adoptive, beloved or never-once-met). Have them share heartily their quirky memories about none other than you, for example, the time your sister cut the nipple off a baby bottle and showed you how to drip milk all over daddy's books. If you can't remember specific childhood memories, feel free to make up a few interesting moments.

18

. . . .

Get A Job

On this date in 1955, Weldon Kees' Plymouth Savoy was found on the north side of the Golden Gate Bridge, the keys in the ignition. Though he'd talked of starting a new life in Mexico, most presumed suicide. Since that day, Kees has increasingly become a cult figure among poets, his poems admired for their earnest intensity and their facility with everyday speech. In one of his poems, Kees describes corporate jobs as *Siberias with bonuses*, places where *the fire roared and died*. Do you now have or did you once have a job where the *phoenix quacked like a goose*? What were you duties? What specifically about the job made you long to call in sick? Write a poem in everyday speech about a job you once had.

19

• •

On Your List

In admiration of Juan Felipe Herrera's poem entitled "187 Reasons Mexicans Can't Cross the Border," write your own list poem using "because" as your refrain word. Examples from Herrera's poem: *Because the north is really south, Because every nacho chip can morph into a Mexican wrestler, Because Pancho Villa's hidden treasure is still in Chihuahua, Because we couldn't clean up Hurricane Katrina, Because we have visions instead of televisions.* Some suggested topic ideas may be: "99 Reasons to Grow Your Own Food," "54 Reasons It's Not Your Fault You're Fat," "88 Ways to Say No without Saying No." For further inspiration, listen to Herrera reading his poem: http://www.youtube.com/watch?v=W8Ben-1n5zQ

JULY

20

· ·

Coined Words

Pick a decade and find out what words were coined. The book, *There's a Word for It: The Explosion of the American Language Since 1900*, available in libraries or online, is a great resource. In today's poem, tell the story of that era through at least six words coined during your chosen decade. For instance, here's a list of words coined in 1930: *zipper, jingle, downgrade, escapist, drive-in, rocketry, mega-universe, schnozzle, schemer.*

21

. . . .

Here's The Report

In celebration of poet Tess Gallagher's birthday, spend some time in the outdoors, even if it means taking a walk to the post office or stepping out to retrieve the mail. Gallagher, reflecting on exploring vast amounts of territory in both the Pacific Northwest and the Ozarks, states "it builds something in you." Whether it's an appreciation for bird song or a fondness for cottonwood fluff, let the natural world build something in you today, then share about it in a poem of ten lines of ten syllables each.

JULY

22

. . . .

We'll Be Driving

I often find my best poems while driving, but only when I pay close attention, viewing road signs, billboards, restaurants, and movie theatre marquees with fresh eyes. Who lives on the street named *Never Give Up Road*? What does a store called *BIGLOTS!* tell us about the age we live in? Wipe the nothing's-new-under-the-sun sand from your eyes, and get into your car (or motorcycle or bike), and make a poem out of what you find.

JULY

23

. . . .

Find A Museum

Michael Kimmelman, *New York Times* art critic, shares with readers why we go to art museums: "and that's what we're looking for when we look at art, no? Something of value, deeper and more meaningful than a name or a number, which cannot be gotten out of a test tube or lab report, which, emotionally speaking, requires an effort on our part. It demands that we look for ourselves." If possible, visit an art museum (virtually counts!), choose a work that speaks to you, and jot down a description, along with one of the following: (1) what you would say to the work of art if you could, (2) what the painting or sculpture would say if it could speak, (3) a fictional explanation of how the work of art came to be.

JULY

24

· ·

Why I Hate The Color Blue

Write a poem in which the title begins with "Why." Examples: "Why I'd Like to Meet My Maker," "Why I Would Never Dye My Hair." In her poem "Why She Would Take Off Her Shoes Before Jumping From The Golden Gate Bridge," Annette Spaulding-Convy writes: *Maybe the water / is a temple* and *She doesn't want // to bring the road's dirt // inside.* Push to move past expected responses to strange and imaginative ones. For extra credit, compose your poem in couplets.

25

· ·

Swearing Off

Write a poem wherein you swear off something or someone. Examples: caffeine, booze, porn, *Sex in the City* reruns, a toxic boyfriend or girlfriend, a drug-addicted child. Tell us specifically (with concrete images) why you are saying goodbye to a bad habit or toxic alliance, then show us how your decision will change your life for the better.

JULY

26

. . . .

Portrait

Write a poem that is a study of a human being in
motion. Describe your chosen person's actions and
imagine their thoughts. Suggestions for whom you
might study: a waitress, a postal worker, a lifeguard, a
conductor, a chef, your mom in the kitchen. Here's an
excerpt from Joyce S. Brown's "The Waitress at
Atwater's" to get you started:

Perhaps
the spilled ketchup
annoys her, or
she sees in the shiny surface
some scene she would rather forget.

JULY

27

. . . .

Grateful / Dread

Ellen Bass tells us, in her poem "Relax," which appeared in *American Poetry Review*, and is available in her book *Like A Beggar* (Copper Canyon Press, 2014):

Bad things are going to happen.
Your tomatoes will grow a fungus
and your cat will get run over.
Someone will leave the bag with the ice cream
melting in the car and throw
your blue cashmere sweater in the drier.

By the end of the poem there's this unctuous description of a strawberry, how *the tiny seeds / crunch between your teeth.* Divide a piece of paper down the middle. Label one side "Things I Dread" and the other "Things I Am Grateful For." After you've brainstormed a list of ten things on each side, write a poem that combines these two opposite poles.

28

. . . .

Pantoum

A pantoum is a poem of any length consisting of four-line stanzas in which the second and fourth lines of each stanza become the first and third lines of the next. The first and last lines are the same. Repetitive actions and/or thoughts make great subjects. Some pantoums repeat lines exactly, while others take liberties, as in this excerpt from Susan Blackwell Ramsey's "Louise Erdrich Learning Ojibiwemowin":

"*Two-thirds of Ojibiwemowin is verbs,*
and nouns aren't male or female, they're living or dead.
(She's learning the language so she'll get the jokes.)
The word for stone, asin, is animate.

If nouns aren't male and female, but living or dead,
What you think you know begins to shift.
Their word for stone, asin, is animate
and that universe came from a conversation of stones.

JULY

29

· ·

New Knowledge

Stanley Kunitz, whose birthday is today, is quoted as saying that "a poet must know everything." Spend some time studying a subject you know little or nothing about, then write a poem using what you've learned. Examples: hummingbirds, rocket science, banana slugs, neuropsychology, barbed-wire fences, shodding horses.

JULY

30

. . . .

Death

Scandinavian poet Henrik Nordbrandt asks in his poem "Cathedral": *Who doesn't want to die / like May rain over the lilacs, / like wild carrots in a ditch?* How would you like to die? How don't you want to die? Do you want to be cremated or buried? If cremated, do you want your remains to be marked, or do you want to have your ashes scattered? Make a list of your preferences, then work them into a poem.

JULY

31

. . . .

Gritty, Gutsy, And Groveling

It's poet Kim Addonizio's birthday. *Booklist*'s Donna Seaman likens Addonizio to a "smoky-voiced chanteuse," a poet who writes about regrets and resignation, pleasure and pain. To celebrate her birthday, write a gritty, gutsy, and/or groveling poem that includes at least six of these words: *stilettos, hangover, whiskey, cigarette, dying, love, begging, naked, jail, dog, hotel.* For extra credit, address the reader.

AUGUST

AUGUST

1

. . . .

Juxtapose Life

On this day in 1960, Chubby Checker released "The Twist" while on this same day in 1936, Adolph Hitler opened the 11th Olympic Games in Berlin. Write a poem that takes two completely different events and juxtaposes them. Find the similarities in the events and connect them in your poem.

AUGUST

2

· ·

Acrostic Place

Walk around your house and find an object you purchased on a trip somewhere. Write the letters of the city where you purchased this item down the left hand column of your page—each letter from the name of the city will begin your first line. For example, if you're writing about a brooch from Paris, the first word in your first line would begin with a "P," the first word in the second line would begin with an "A" and so on until you've spelled out the city name. Now, write a poem that incorporates the item and deals with an event that took place during that trip.

AUGUST

3

. . . .

In The Surreal World

Close your eyes and imagine yourself holding five things in your hand: a person, a building, a weapon, and two other items of your choosing. Write a poem that incorporates all five items. For extra credit, use one item three times throughout the poem.

AUGUST

4

. . . .

I Want A New Drug

Write a poem about a drug that doesn't exist. Give it
an abstract name like "Violence" or something unique
like "Milk Money." What does this drug do? Is it more
medicinal or something more like LSD? Is it sold
legally or illegally? Can this drug save the world or ruin
it? Begin the poem, *That August. . .*

AUGUST

5

. . . .

Words Inside Words

Today is poet Wendell Berry's birthday. Born in 1934, Berry is known for his writing as well as his activism. In his poem, "A Homecoming," he writes, *Wild /in the wilderness.* . . Make a list of larger words (or compound words) that contains stem words (or unintentional words) in them. For example, your list may include:

dark/darkness

faith/faithful

some/time/sometime

friend/ship/end/friendship, etc.

Write a poem where various forms of the same word appear, and/or where the stem of a word and its suffix appear in the same sentence. Use repetition liberally while continuing to look for words inside words.

AUGUST

6

· ·

Atomic Memories

From the New York Times: "On Aug. 6, 1945, the
United States dropped an atomic bomb on Hiroshima,
Japan, that instantly killed an estimated 66,000 people in
the first use of a nuclear weapon in warfare." Write a
poem in memory of an event. The event can either be
a celebration or a tragedy.

AUGUST

7

. . . .

Make It Happen

Make up five intriguing events that have never happened to you, such as "Was given a tour of the White House where I ran into the President in Abe Lincoln's bedroom," or "Skydived with a bouquet of irises." Choose your favorite moment that never happened and write a poem about it. For extra credit, write a poem about all the made-up events you wrote down.

AUGUST

8

. . . .

What's Up, Doc?

Think of a favorite cartoon character. Write a poem
where that character gives you some smart (or not so
smart) advice. For example, maybe Homer Simpson
wants to discuss healthy eating. Or Elmer Fudd wants
to talk with you about gun safety. It can be a cartoon
character from your childhood, a movie, or a currently-
airing animated show.

AUGUST

9

. . . .

City Nature

On this day in 1854, Henry David Thoreau published *Walden*. Write a poem that uses the names of two regional trees in your area and two types of flowers or groundcover. Have the poem begin in an urban environment and end in a wooded setting. For extra credit, include a name of a regional bird, shrub, and amphibian.

AUGUST

10

. . . .

In Six

There's an urban legend that novelist Ernest Hemingway was dared to write a story that was under ten words long. He used six words and wrote: "For Sale: baby shoes. Never worn." Write a poem about the history of a relationship where each line is comprised of only six words.

AUGUST

11

. . . .

Headliners

Find a newspaper or go to your favorite Internet news source and write a poem inspired from one of the headlines. For extra credit, choose a headline about something specific and write a poem that has little to do with that topic.

AUGUST

12

. . . .

Meteor Middle

We are in the middle of the Perseid meteor shower.
Write a poem that includes a celestial event and features
an explosion or some sort of light show in the middle
of the poem. For extra credit, bring your pen, paper,
and flashlight outside and write a poem beneath the
Perseid meteor shower.

AUGUST

13

. . . .

Sharpshooters

Today is the birthday of Annie Oakley, American sharpshooter, born in 1860. Write a poem that has either a gun and/or a woman doing a job you might not expect (rancher, construction worker, football player, plumber, etc.).

AUGUST

14

. . . .

Dog Days

Write a poem that features a type of dog, such as a dachshund, golden retriever, or Jack Russell terrier. Ensure the poem does not become precious or over-sentimentalized by writing the poem from the point of view of a distant observer. For extra credit, write the poem in the voice of the dog.

AUGUST

15

. . . .

Woodstock Inspiration

On this day in 1969, the Woodstock Music and Art Festival opened. Listen to the music of Janis Joplin; Jimi Hendrix; the Grateful Dead; Crosby, Stills, Nash, & Young; Joe Cocker; Joan Baez; or any of the other performers who appeared that weekend and write a poem inspired by one (or several) of their songs. If you are unable to listen to their music today, write a poem about a concert you've attended.

AUGUST

16

· ·

The History Of Names

Research the names in your family to see what they
mean. For example, Delaney means "from the alder
grove," Russell means "redhead" and LeBlanc means
"white." Write a poem that incorporates the definitions
or the history of certain names into your poem. For
extra credit, make up definitions for names you've
invented, such as "Mothberry, meaning: to flutter
between fruit."

AUGUST

17

. . . .

A Quote Can Start
A Thousand Poems

Spend ten minutes meditating on the quote by Wallace
Stevens, "The poet is the priest of the invisible." When
you open your eyes, write down the words and images
that came to you. Now write a poem using those
images.

AUGUST

18

. . . .

Where You Are Now

Stand up and take three steps in any direction. Look around and note three different items, the color of the wall (or whatever is in front of you), and note what is above you. Imagine that you have just arrived at this place from another country and are homesick. Write a poem that includes what you see, how you feel, and what you miss about your home country.

AUGUST

19

. . . .

Linked Haiku

In the U.S., haiku is usually taught in school as a three-line poem with a 5-7-5 syllable count. Write a haiku about your favorite blooming flower of August or any favorite tree or vine. Use the last line of your first haiku as the first line of your second haiku. Use the last line of your second haiku as the first line of your third haiku.

AUGUST

20

· ·

Dream Syllabics

Write a poem about a dream that has seven syllables in each line. If you can't remember your dream, ask a friend, lover, spouse, or child about a dream s/he recently had and write a poem about that. For extra credit, write this poem immediately after waking up in the morning.

AUGUST

21

. . . .

Hawaii Without The Trees
And Water

On this date in 1959, Hawaii became the 50th state in the U.S. Write a poem about Hawaii, traveling to Hawaii, or a previous trip you've taken there without mentioning the ocean or palm trees. Incorporate the theme of loss into your poem.

AUGUST

22

. . . .

Coloring Outside The Lines

Choose a color. Now write a poem only using images of that color. For example, if you chose white, your poem might include clouds, snow, yogurt, angels, paper, ping-pong balls, or plastic bags. The poem may or may not evoke an emotion associated with your chosen color.

AUGUST

23

. . . .

Nature's Gift

Walk outside and find three natural items. Make a list of human-made items these natural items resemble. For example, if you brought in a pinecone, write down *grenade* or *brown golf ball*. Now, write a poem that incorporates all the natural items and the human-made items they resemble. For extra credit, have each item appear in a very different setting from where you originally found it.

AUGUST

24

. . . .

Things They Never Did

Write a poem that features a famous person or a family member doing or saying something surprising or out of character. For example, George Washington playing Skee-Ball or Emily Dickinson throwing a block party. What you make them do does not have to be true; just be creative.

AUGUST

25

. . . .

Odd Listings

Write a poem that includes five unusual desserts, two types of tools, a specific kind of tree, and a famous outlaw. Let the poem go wherever it wants to go, no matter how odd. For extra credit, mention a personal ad, a letter to Saint Jude, or the name of your first pet.

AUGUST

26

. . . .

Bad Day

Write a poem about a bad day. Consider adding something to do with an elevator, a microwave, an exploding can of soda, a spilled glass of wine, a flat tire, or a lost briefcase. Bad day poems are a great opportunity to incorporate the comic into your writing. Look at the event as if you, personally, are not having the bad time, aiming to find the humor in the errors of the day.

AUGUST

27

· ·

Secrets For Friends

Write a poem to a close friend and tell her/him something s/he doesn't know about you. If this friend knows everything, make something up. The poem can be in the form of a postcard or letter. For extra credit, mail the finished poem to the person you wrote about.

AUGUST

28

. . . .

Taking Dictation From The Dead

Close your eyes and imagine a poet (living or dead).
Think about everything you know about this poet.
Imagine him or her sitting down with you on a
comfortable sofa. Now, ask the poet to dictate a poem
to you and write down everything s/he says.

AUGUST

29

. . . .

Times 29

Write a poem that repeats a word of your choosing twenty-nine times. For extra credit, have the poem be twenty-nine lines and allow the word to appear in every line except the title.

AUGUST

30

. . . .

Highway Life

On this date in 1965, Bob Dylan released the album, *Highway 61 Revisited.* Write a poem where you visit a favorite street or highway near where you live. If possible, ask a friend to drive you up and down that street a few times so you can take notes to use in your poem, or if possible, spend an hour walking the street with notebook in hand, jotting down all you experience.

AUGUST

31

. . . .

Summer's End

Write a poem that includes three things you saw or did this summer. Write the poem in a dream-sequence, moving from one event to the other. Keep the flow of the poem loose and conversational, so you can casually move from one topic to another.

SEPTEMBER

SEPTEMBER

1

. . . .

Bus Station, Train Station, Airport

Write a poem that takes place in a bus/train station or airport. In Jim Harrison's poem "Sunlight," he shares a moment of seeing the sun peek through clouds for a few seconds, comparing it to our brief time here on Earth. In your poem, describe an image that allows you to make grand statements about time, mortality, the cosmos, etc. For more inspiration, read Harrison's poem "Sunlight" at:

http://writersalmanac.publicradio.org/index.php?date=2012/08/09

SEPTEMBER

2

. . . .

Witness To Racism

In honor of the thirty Chinese immigrant miners murdered on this date in 1885 by white miners in the Rock Springs Massacre due to racial tensions related to a labor dispute, write a poem that candidly relates a tale of racist behavior. Examples: being told a racist joke, viewing derogatory depictions of a given race, being discriminated against (treated a certain way) because of your ethnic heritage.

SEPTEMBER

3

. . . .

No Life On Mars

On this date in 1976, the Viking 2 unmanned spacecraft took the first close-up color pictures of the surface of Mars. Write a poem about the frantic search to find water (and perhaps living creatures) on Mars. As there is plenty of life already here on Earth that needs attending to, your poem may or may not take on a cynical tone.

SEPTEMBER

4

. . . .

Kodak Moment

On this date in 1888, George Eastman patented the first roll film camera for Kodak. Write a series of short poems that each present a snapshot description of a larger subject. To get inspired, scroll through a virtual or actual box of old photos. Find a series of shots that resonate with you—perhaps from your last vacation—then write a few lines about each snapshot.

SEPTEMBER

5

. . . .

Ecopoetics

Poets Brenda Hillman, Camille Dungy, and Joshua Corey write about the natural world without romanticizing it. Poets who write ecopoetry espouse an ecological imperative, writing poems that share their connection to the natural world, expressing a personal responsibility toward it. Read a sampling of ecopoetic poems, then try your hand at writing a poem that confronts climate change, environmental degradation, habitat destruction, and/or forest mismanagement straight on. If you get stuck, try putting some of these words into your poem: *cage, habitat, dead, altered, destabilized, remnant, margins, mutilated.*

SEPTEMBER

6

· ·

The Future Of Poetry

What will the poem of the future look like? Will words function as signifiers in five hundred years, or will they be merely decorative? Will the point of the poem one thousand years from now be to make no sense at all? Write a poem in a style you envision future readers will find praiseworthy.

SEPTEMBER

7

. . . .

Aubade

In celebration of Dame Edith Sitwell's birthday on this date in 1887, "aubade" yourself (a morning love song or poem about two lovers separating at dawn). Instead of falling into overwrought clichés about passionate lovers disentangling, make the lovers non-human creatures, such as mayflies or lightning bugs bidding adieu after a long and passionate night. For more inspiration: you can read Sitwell's poem "Aubade" at: www.allpoetry.com/poem/8519135-Aubade-by-Dame_Edith_Sitwell

SEPTEMBER

8

· ·

Temper, Temper!

Slowly lose your temper in today's poem. Your poem should begin in calm and end in fury, rage, and/or tears. Think Elizabeth Bishop's "The Art of Losing" but instead of lost things, your poem will unravel with one annoyance, frustration, slight, problem at a time until the explosive crescendo ending. Feel free to curse the perpetrator, hail epithets at the inanimate objects messing with you. You might also find it in your heart to express empathy for those who have committed unspeakable crimes.

SEPTEMBER

9

. . . .

I Come From

In celebration of the birth of Sonia Sanchez on this day in 1934, write a poem in which each line begins *I come from*. The "I" in the poem, should not be you but a specific person (living or dead): Elvis Presley, Taylor Swift, your mother, that homeless person you pass each morning on the way to work. Make the voice as authentic as possible, striving to capture how the person might speak (accent, dialect, word choice), as well as his or her unique poetic voice.

SEPTEMBER

10

. . . .

You Do Not Have To Be Good

In honor of the birthday of Mary Oliver (b. 1935) and her poem "Wild Geese," which begins *You do not have to be good*, write a poem where you tell your reader what he or she does not have to be or do in order to succeed, win favor, or get into heaven. Perhaps she doesn't have to keep a clean kitchen or shine her husband's shoes. Be specific about the tasks or self-grooming not necessary for a ticket to paradise. For more inspiration: read Oliver's poem "Wild Geese" at:

http://writersalmanac.publicradio.org/?date=2002/06/21

SEPTEMBER

11

· ·

9/11

On this date in 2001, terrorists manned four commercial airliners, crashing them into New York's World Trade Center towers, the Pentagon, and into a field in Shanksville, PA. Over 3,000 people perished during the deadliest act of violence ever to occur on American soil. In 2009, the United States Congress declared September 11 as a national day of service and remembrance. *The New York Times* online has obituaries alphabetically arranged, as well as ongoing stories about family members of the dead. After reading a few profiles and stories, write a poem about one or more victims of the 9/11 tragedy. If you do not have an Internet connection, write a poem about a personal tragedy, the death of a family member, a loss, or an accident.

SEPTEMBER

12

. . . .

You're Not Going To Believe This, But

For today's assignment, choose an historical figure from the Pre-Industrial age, and share what's happened since his/her death. For instance, have a chat with Napoleon about nuclear warheads, a peasant farmer about wind-powered turbines, or sit down with a Wright brother to discuss the SST. Feel free to make this a humorous poem if you are inclined.

SEPTEMBER

13

. . . .

Poking Fun At Metaphor

For today's poem, compare two things ("my stomach rumbled like a Shiite car bomb" or "she was soft in the belly like an earthworm"), but then poke fun at metaphor by extending the metaphor until it becomes surreal. Examples: "but she was also like an earthworm in that she had no legs, arms, or ears" or "Also, like a Shiite bomb, my life had become terroristic in its lack of moral direction." In other words, have fun playing with metaphor, seeing how far you can push your poem into wacky and absurd pronouncements.

SEPTEMBER

14

· ·

How The Pope Gets Chosen

Write a "How To" that provides directions for something your reader will not likely ever do. Examples: "How to Vacuum a Forest" or "How to be a Good President." Create memorable and striking imagery while devising outlandish lies as James Tate does in his poem "How the Pope Gets Chosen." For more inspiration, listen to Tate's poem at: http://www.poets.org/viewmedia.php/prmMID/ 21460 and following Tate's lead, aim to be surreal, absurd, funny, and disinclined to tell the truth.

SEPTEMBER

15

. . . .

But I Digress

Write a poem that changes subjects at least three times. You may use stanza breaks to indicate a leap, or the words "But I digress." Whether or not you return to your original subject is up to you, but try not to tie up loose ends. Experiment with how disparate and unrelated each subject is from the other, but sneak in a less unifying theme, such as the color red.

SEPTEMBER

16

. . . .

I Don't Like It

Write a persona poem in the voice of someone you find distasteful in some way. He or she might tell racist jokes, be a poacher or a misogynist, a skinhead, or share different views than you about climate change, equal rights, privacy rights, etc. Strive to use words and create a tone that accurately depicts this offensive individual.

SEPTEMBER

17

. . . .

The Happy Genius Of My Household

In honor of William Carlos Williams, born on this date in 1883, write a poem in which your speaker revels in his or her flawed, yet brilliant body and being. In his poem, "Danse Russe," although Williams is known for his strong ties to imagism, he is concerned about specific images (sun, mist, trees), but also intent on creating a poem of exuberant self-love. You might also turn to Walt Whitman for inspiration. Read "Danse Russe" online at:

www.poetryfoundation.org/poem/175782

SEPTEMBER

18

. . . .

Water, Water Everywhere

For today's poem, focus on the topic of water. If you cannot get yourself to a pond, lake, river, stream, pool or puddle today, turn on your faucet and observe how water comes streaming out. Jot down memories relating to water: canoeing at summer camp, purifying water on a backpacking trip, being thirsty after recess, etc. As you compose your water poem, consider including one or more of the following words: *aqueous, liquefaction, ripple, splash.*

SEPTEMBER

19

. . . .

Sweep Away The Scaffolding

To commemorate the patenting of the carpet sweeper by Melville Bissell on this date in 1876, today's poem prompt asks you to take a poem you enjoy and write or type out each line, leaving a few inches of space between each line. Once you've done this, freewrite (or riff) for two to three minutes off each line of your chosen poem. Finally, remove the borrowed poem and voila, you have a poem for today.

SEPTEMBER

20

. . . .

The Things

In honor of the poet Donald Hall, born on this date in 1928, write a poem inspired by Hall's "The Things." Hall's poem calls attention to the *valueless, unforgettable / detritus* we humans collect and cherish, odds and ends our loved ones will likely throw away after we've departed. Following Hall's lead, make a list of items of little monetary value that you cherish for sentimental reasons, then choose one item from your list and write a short poem in which you describe this favorite item. Share how you acquired it and posit where this object will end up after you're dead. "The Things" can be found at:

http://www.poetryfoundation.org/poetrymagazin e/article/146874

SEPTEMBER

21

· ·

Cleaning Out The Gecko Cage

We all have routine tasks we tend to put off—changing the oil, mowing the lawn, or cleaning out the gecko cage. Today's poem asks you to perform a menial task (weeding, washing the car, organizing your closet) and write in detail about not only what you did, but what you were thinking about while you did it. For instance, what did the gecko look like? What did it feel like to pick it up? Try not to rush through your task, but instead treat it like a form of meditation (chopping wood and carrying water).

SEPTEMBER

22

. . . .

First Word, Same Word

Choose a word and make it the title and/or first word of today's poem. Continue making it the first word of each line of your poem. Words such as *if, because,* and *and* work well, but consider challenging yourself by using a proper or place name, or a word with many meanings. Examples: *go, take, run, stand, get, turn, fall.* See if you can make your poem at least ten lines long.

SEPTEMBER

23

. . . .

Bless You

Write a poem in the form of a blessing. Each line should begin *May you...* Examples: *May you witness the simple act of placing old cans and bottles in their proper place* and *May a bald-faced hornet buzz by you, disinterested.* After you've written at least twenty lines, end your poem with an image of welcomed silence.

SEPTEMBER

24

. . . .

I've Looked At Clouds

Go outside and observe the daytime sky. If there are clouds, what do they resemble—turtles, gerbils, a spread-eagle angel? If the sky is cloudless, write about the emotions it provokes. Then write a poem about the sky that has nothing to do with weather.

SEPTEMBER

25

· ·

Nonsense

In honor of the birthday of Shel Silverstein (1930), write a nonsense poem in the manner of "Ickle Me, Pickle Me, Tickle Me Too," available online through a web search or on YouTube. Make sure your poem contains at least one invented word, plenty of end rhyme, and a repeating (and silly) refrain line at the end of each stanza.

SEPTEMBER

26

. . . .

T.S. Eliot

In honor of the birthday of poet Thomas Stearns Eliot on this day in 1888, write a poem loosely based on the life of the poet. Use Wikipedia and other websites to garner facts, but make sure to fabricate parts of his life. For instance, it's a well-known fact that Eliot adored cheese, so perhaps in your poem he works for a time in a Brie factory.

SEPTEMBER

27

. . . .

Migration

Write a poem that deals in some way with relocation. Your poem might be literally about animals or birds heading south, but it could also focus on metaphorical movements to warmer climes, fleeing a gelid employer, roommate, or romantic relation.

SEPTEMBER

28

. . . .

Jargon Talking

After doing a bit of research about the unique language of a specific profession or activity (horseracing, knitting or quilting, construction, finance), write a poem that incorporates a particular jargon. Example: if you chose horseracing, your poem might contain the following jargon: *bottle, carpet, blanket finish, also ran, bat, bug boy, cuppy*. Consider using the language metaphorically writing about a totally unrelated subject using your chosen jargon.

SEPTEMBER

29

. . . .

Cliché Mash-Up

Write a poem that plays around with clichés, tired
phrases, or familiar quotations, and/or famous
sayings/lines from poems or songs. Consider using one
or more of these tropes to weave together a poem of
off-kilter or misheard phrases ("In the ear of our Lord"
or "Free alas") with phrases such as: *I thought you said,
Didn't you say, I could swear you said.*

SEPTEMBER

30

. . . .

O Pile Of White Shirts

In honor of the birthday of W.S. Merwin (b. 1927),
write a poem inspired by "Night of the Shirts."
Compose your poem in a dreamy, stream-of-
consciousness style, omitting capitalization (except for
the first letter of the first word of the poem) and
punctuation. Address it to a domestic item or items—
ironing board, dishwasher, cutting board, etc. You can
find "Night of the Shirts" at:

http://www.poetryfoundation.org/poem/171869.

OCTOBER

OCTOBER

1

· ·

The Full Moon

You may have noticed the harvest moon of September, but October with its large O looks like a moon. Write a poem about the moon using multiple O words. Words with capital O's look even better. Make a list of some words that begin with O and go go go.

OCTOBER

2

. . . .

The Beginning Of Fall

What does fall look like in your part of the world?
What are the subtle changes you are beginning to see?
Write a poem that explores the subtleness of change. If
you need a start, begin the poem with the line, *I almost
saw...*

OCTOBER

3

· ·

The Marriage

Write a poem that combines two completely different things—sci-fi and mountain biking, horror movies and a tea party, fencing and Apple Brown Betty. Allow the poem to branch out into different directions then return and reunite. For extra credit, have either a marriage or a divorce included in the poem.

OCTOBER

4

. . . .

Sputnik!

On this day in 1957, the former Soviet Union launched
Sputnik. Write a poem about outer space, the universe,
and/or space history that never happened. Maybe
invent your own planet from an emotion—call it Planet
Depression or Planet Love—and create your own alien
landscape. Be as wild or refined as you wish.

OCTOBER

5

. . . .

Breakfast At Your House

In 1961, *Breakfast at Tiffany's* was released. Write a poem about breakfast at your house. Make sure to include the specific details about what you eat or drink, as well as the pace of the morning. To keep this poem from becoming clichéd, consider including the following words: *diamond, Holly Golightly, Moon River, Truman Capote, Audrey Hepburn, window-shopping.*

OCTOBER

6

. . . .

Pop-Art In An American Supermarket

In 1964, a pop-art exhibit featuring Andy Warhol, Roy Lichtenstein, and other artists was featured at the Bianchini Gallery in New York City. Write your own pop-art poem about a moment in a supermarket. For research, spend some time in the aisles with a notebook and write down what you hear and see. Use unique names of products, popular culture, and feature the unusual in your poem.

OCTOBER

7

· ·

Nevermore

Edgar Allan Poe died on this day in 1857. Poe was famous for his long narrative poem "The Raven" with its line *quoth the raven, "Nevermore."* Write a poem in a narrative style that has a repetitive line or refrain. Your poem can be inspired by Poe's poem or not.

OCTOBER

8

· ·

A Small Event Began It

On this day in 1871, the Great Chicago Fire killed 300 people and left 100,000 people homeless. The legend is that Mrs. O'Leary's cow kicked over a lantern, beginning the huge blaze. Write a poem where a smaller incident creates a much larger incident. It can do with nature, such as an oil spill or a forest fire, or perhaps an argument between two people. You can make it surreal—let an unopened jar of pickles collapse a universe or a spilled glass of orange juice flood a town. Let your imagination spin a few tales (make a list!) and write from that.

OCTOBER

9

. . . .

Imagine

John Lennon and his son, Sean Lennon, were both born on this day. Write a poem about a parent/child relationship, whether your own or as an observer. In your poem, choose an image you feel best represents the relationship (two fighting tigers, a pair of lily pads in a pond, two robins in a maple tree, etc.) and have that image reoccur in different ways throughout the poem.

OCTOBER

10

. . . .

Tuxedo City

In this day in 1886, the tuxedo was introduced by
Griswold Lorillard to the Tuxedo Club in Tuxedo Park,
New York. For your poem, choose a city whose name
you like and rename something in that city's honor.
For example, if you choose Walla Walla, Washington, as
your city, invent the Walla Walla Windbreaker or the
Walla Walla Wristwatch. If you choose Humptulips,
Washington, use it to create Humptulips Lingerie or
Humptulips Tulips. If you choose San Jose, California,
create San Jose Hosiery. Feel free to make up as many
new items as you like, using them to inspire a poem.

OCTOBER

11

. . . .

SNL Through The Years

In 1975, *Saturday Night Live* (SNL) debuted on NBC. Write a poem that is set after midnight that includes either an SNL personality, such as Tina Fey or Chevy Chase, or a reference to the SNL skit characters, such as the Coneheads, Doug and Wendy Whiner, Wayne and Garth, Landshark, etc. Feel free to slip in any reoccurring words or phrases from SNL shows over the years: cowbell, superstar, marvelous, never mind, or live from New York.

OCTOBER

12

. . . .

Picnic In The Wrong Season

Write a poem about going on a picnic on a rainy day, a stormy day, during a hurricane, a snowstorm, or some other weather event not conducive to sitting outside. For a twist, have the poem include either a positive outcome or a positive moment during what might be viewed as a terrible day.

OCTOBER

13

. . . .

Who's Afraid Of Any Author?

On this day in 1962, Edward Albee's play, *Who's Afraid of Virginia Woolf?* opened on Broadway. Write a poem where you take the name of an author and have it reoccur in your poem in surprising ways. If you don't know where to begin, use the image of walking into an old or used bookstore and reaching for a book.

OCTOBER

14

. . . .

Interruptions Please

Write a poem where you have a speaker who interrupts your poem as it goes along. For example, if you're writing: "She spent the days of December reading," have the speaker butt in afterwards with the question: *Proust?* This "second voice" in the poem can be a critic, questioner, or someone who enjoys commenting. Put the speaker's interruptions in italics, so they stand out from the actual poem. Start the poem with "It's easy to live with nothing…"

OCTOBER

15

· ·

I Do Love Lucy

In 1951, when *I Love Lucy* debuted on CBS, Lucy and Ricky smoked throughout their sitcom. Write a poem where you create a scene of something that was once okay, but today is no longer the social norm. Whether it's driving your kids around without seatbelts, a common occurrence before the 1970s, or three-martini lunches, write a poem that includes something that is no longer acceptable.

OCTOBER

16

. . . .

Ever Been To Paris?

In 1793, Marie Antoinette was beheaded two and a half weeks before her thirty-eighth birthday during the French Revolution. Write a poem that imagines a parade of Marie Antoinettes or another famous French figure walking down a street in the city of Paris, Wisconsin (population 754).

OCTOBER

17

· ·

Money Matters

Write a poem about something you consider "priceless," but try to put a price on it. Imagine what you'd get for your love if you traded it in a pawn shop. How much would you get for that memory from your honeymoon? What if there were a gold coin for the experience of complete bliss—what would it look like?

OCTOBER

18

. . . .

Telephone Game

In 1892, New York and Chicago were connected for the first time by a long-distance telephone line. For this poem, we're going to do a poetic play on the kids' "Telephone Game" where you whisper something to one person in the circle and watch it change as it moves from child to child. Write a first line to a poem about anything you like. Now take this line and morph it a bit; that line will become the first line of your second stanza. For example, if you wrote, "I dream in color about cantaloupes," your next line might be, "I dream in color, but can't elope." Now, take that new second line and morph it a bit more. This will be the first line of your third stanza. Continue to do this two more times, so you have five similar (but different!) lines, write a poem where each of these lines begins each of your five stanzas.

OCTOBER

19

. . . .

The Fake Version Of Your Life

Write a poem where you make up a completely
different history for yourself or where you write about
something you never did. Think specifically of all the
things you have wanted to do, or things you'd never do
because they frighten you. If you're afraid to fly, write a
poem about how you went skydiving. If you've always
wanted to see Rome, write a poem in which you visit
that city.

OCTOBER

20

. . . .

100 Words On Dewey

Write a poem of exactly 100 words on the library's Dewey Decimal System or on its creator, Melvil Dewey. Feel free to use titles of books, alliteration, and/or alphabetization throughout your poem. You may have to do some research online or at your library to find the right details for your poem.

OCTOBER

21

· ·

I'm So Dizzy

On this day in 1917, jazz trumpeter Dizzy Gillespie was born. Write a poem about feeling dizzy after listening to jazz. Some titles from Dizzy Gillespie songs that might be good images are: "Salt Peanuts," "Second Balcony Jump," "Bebop," "Victory Ball," or "Overtime."

OCTOBER

22

. . . .

Over-Punctuate Me

Write a poem where you take one punctuation mark
(period, comma, dash, question mark, exclamation
mark, etc.) and use it repeatedly throughout the poem.
For extra credit, have the poem be about something
related to the punctuation mark you chose. For
example, if you choose a comma, the poem might be
about pausing to consider something, or if you chose a
question mark, the poem could be about a question.

OCTOBER

23

. . . .

Late Night TV

Johnny Carson was born today in 1925. Write a poem that opens like a late night TV monologue. Write directly to your reader about something that happened in the news as if you are speaking to that person directly. Feel free to use any images, words, props, or imagined camera angles from your favorite late night talk show. For extra credit, mention a late night TV host: Conan O'Brien, Jimmy Fallon, David Letterman, or Jimmy Kimmel.

OCTOBER

24

. . . .

What Falls

Write a poem that explores something falling. Leaves might be the obvious idea this time of year, but what about rock-a-bye baby on the treetop, a falling heart rate or blood pressure, falling in love or falling out of love. Make a list of all the things that fall and write a poem about one or more of them.

OCTOBER

25

. . . .

Picasso It

Today is the birthday of Pablo Picasso, born in 1881. To celebrate Picasso's abstract artwork, write a poem about something abstract (love, kindness, hatred, soul, afterlife, etc.) using very concrete images, visual elements, and colors. Or ask yourself: *If your poem were a Picasso painting, what would it look like?*

OCTOBER

26

. . . .

Holiday Upon Holiday

In the stores there are Halloween decorations with Thanksgiving decorations right next to Christmas decorations. Write a poem that either has the same event—a fight, a proposal, something breaking—happening on three different holidays or include three different holiday images in the same poem.

OCTOBER

27

· ·

Ms. Plath And Her Fruit

Sylvia Plath was born on this date in 1932. Take the first line of her poem, "Blackberrying" and use it for the first line (or title) of your poem: *Nobody in the lane, and nothing, nothing but blackberries.* Feel free to change the word "blackberries" to another noun of your choosing, now write a poem about that noun instead. For extra credit, include the word "blackberries" in the last line of the poem or reference Sylvia Plath in the title.

OCTOBER

28

. . . .

Leaves

Go outside and find a leaf on the ground. Or find a few of them. Imagine writing a love letter, goodbye letter, or note to a friend on that leaf. What would you write? If you could only write one word on that leaf to hand to them, what would it be? Write a poem about what you imagined.

OCTOBER

29

. . . .

Superstitious

Write a poem that includes one or more superstitions. Whether you are afraid of black cats crossing your path or of walking under ladders, pick a superstition you have or someone you know has and write about it. Or make up your own superstition (if you see a dead mason bee in your bathroom, you'll have three years of bad luck) and write about that.

OCTOBER

30

. . . .

Spooky

Write a poem that includes a ghost. It can be a friendly ghost or a mischievous one. Maybe the ghost is trying to tell you something. What does it say? If the ghost is a dead relative or friend, interview him or her in your poem. Have the ghost do something unexpected, or write your poem about a person, and at the very end, reveal that he or she is actually a spirit.

OCTOBER

31

· ·

All Hallow's Eve

Write a poem about a specific moment that could happen on Halloween. It could be about stealing a pumpkin, walking through a graveyard, or giving out candy to trick-or-treaters. Pay attention to specific details, sounds, or sights that might be present on this holiday.

NOVEMBER

NOVEMBER

1

. . . .

All Saints' Day

Write a poem that includes visits from three saints.
You can research saints on the Internet and choose
your favorite, or make a list of your obsessions and
create a saint from that. Write a poem to the Saint of
Poets, the Saint of Birds, or make up your own saint.
The Saint of the Internet, perhaps? The Saint of
Broken Violins? Feel free to use one or more real or
invented saints in your poem.

NOVEMBER

2

. . . .

Leftover Candy

Write a poem that uses the names of as many types of candy or candy bar names you can think of. Feel free to research to find names from the past—Charleston Chews, Necco Wafers, candy cigarettes. See what memories they bring up for you or invent your own. Have the poem be about gain or increase.

NOVEMBER

3

. . . .

What's The Weather Out There?

In many parts of America, November is known for its crazy weather. Walk outside right now and experience the weather. Bring a notebook and take notes of what you hear, see, and smell. Now, write a poem where the weather plays a significant role in changing something, whether an event or a landscape.

NOVEMBER

4

· ·

Weddings "R" Us

On this day in 1842, Abraham Lincoln married Mary Todd in Springfield, Illinois, so today's assignment is to write a wedding poem. It can either be an historical poem or one about two people whom we would never imagine getting married. Or if you like, write a poem about a surprise event at a wedding.

NOVEMBER

5

. . . .

Three-Ring Circus

Write a poem in the form of a three-ring circus—create
three sections each with something unique happening
in each section. To help the poem stay connected, have
a word, color, or unique phrase reappear in each
section. Make a list of three events that *seem* to have
nothing to do with each other—playing tennis in a field
of wildflowers, memorizing the moons of Jupiter, and
taking the subway to work—and write a poem that
connects them.

NOVEMBER

6

. . . .

Find A Book, Any Book

Pick up the closest book to you, no matter what it is. Turn to page fifteen, go down seven lines. Have that line be the title of your poem (or use it as your opening line). For extra credit, use the title of the book you chose your line from somewhere in your poem.

NOVEMBER

7

. . . .

Reduce / Reuse / Recycle

Choose a poem you've written over the last year that you really don't like. Go through and pick out your favorite words or images from that poem. Use those words and images in a new poem that you write today. Have this poem be about something entirely different than the poem you took the images from.

NOVEMBER

8

. . . .

Dear Constellation

Write a poem to your favorite constellation or look up
constellations until you find one with a name, shape, or
meaning you love. You will notice in your research that
some constellations belong to specific constellation
families such as the Zodiac, the Hercules Family, or the
Orion Family. For extra credit, choose a constellation
family and write a poem with as many references to the
constellations in a specific family as you can.

NOVEMBER

9

. . . .

Holy Poetry-Writing, Batman

Write a poem that includes a favorite comic book character or reference to a superhero or fictional cartoon evildoer. Have the poem be about something that has nothing to do with comic books. Feel free to have the comic book hero walk into a party and let the adventure unfold.

NOVEMBER

10

. . . .

Sesame Street And Muppet Man

On this day in 1969, Sesame Street premiered on PBS. Write a poem in which characters from Sesame Street keep knocking on your front door, your bathroom door, or keep calling you to ask for something. What do these characters want from you? How do you respond? Alternatively, if you were a muppet, what would your character look and act like? What is your muppet name? Write a poem that explores what it's like being a puppet.

NOVEMBER

11

· ·

Veterans Day

In honor of Veterans Day, write a poem to or about a veteran. To avoid falling into cliché, write about a veteran doing something completely normal—grocery shopping or pumping gas. Aim to show something about this veteran without mentioning war, guns, or a bombing.

NOVEMBER

12

. . . .

Found On The Page

Pick up a magazine or newspaper and open to any page.
Now close your eyes and put your finger down
somewhere on the page. Use whatever your finger
lands on in your poem. If you land on a phrase or
word, use that. If you land on an advertising image, use
that. Feel free to do this more than once as you
continue your poem.

NOVEMBER

13

. . . .

What You Wanted To Say

Write a poem that begins with the line *I wanted to say...*
Write about something you either didn't get a chance to
say or want to say now. It can be about something
poignant such as what you would have said to a loved
one before s/he died, or something trivial such as
telling a date you would love to see *Steel Magnolias* when
you really want to see *Rambo*.

NOVEMBER

14

. . . .

Teach Us

Write a poem that teaches the reader about something. It can be how to make a certain dish or change a tire. Have this "teaching" happen throughout the poem, but have the poem be about something else entirely. Maybe you're thinking about a lost love as you make soup or maybe you're going on a trip while you teach us the best way to pack a suitcase. See what you can teach the reader when you write the poem about something other than what is being taught.

NOVEMBER

15

. . . .

Ms. O'Keeffe's Larger
Than Life Flowers

On this day in 1887, painter Georgia O'Keeffe was born. As an artist, she created numerous paintings of flowers, bones, and the New Mexico landscape. She was known for painting flowers so huge they covered the canvas. Choose something small—a key, an insect, a coin, a tooth—and write about it in a large way. Over-exaggerate your images, making your small object seem larger than life.

NOVEMBER

16

. . . .

Mini Abecedarian Poem

In an abecedarian poem, every line begins with A, B, C, D, etc. Write a mini-abecedarian poem where each word in the poem is in alphabetical order. For example, the first line of a mini-abecedarian poem could be: *Another big cactus dies entertainingly. Forget giving. Help invent...* or *Autumn birds can desire eggs from groceries...* See if you can write an entire poem this way. Don't worry too much about making sense, just see what new images or lines you can invent.

NOVEMBER

17

. . . .

Your Own Bookstore

On this date in 1919, Sylvia Beach first opened her
bookstore, Shakespeare & Co. in Paris. If you were
going to name a bookstore, what would you call it?
Write a poem where something is found in this
imagined bookstore. Or imagine hosting an historical
dinner party in your bookstore. What poets and writers
(dead or living) would attend? What would they say to
each other?

NOVEMBER

18

· ·

Sounds And How They Repeat

Write the first line of a poem about a something you hope to find. Count in three syllables and whatever sound you land on, repeat that sound in the next lines of the poems. For example, if you begin your poem, *I find diamonds when I'm not searching...* count in three syllables to the "di" sound and repeat it in each line of the poem. Your next line could be, *Maybe I'm dying...* or *Diners are filled with shiny objects.* See how this repetition forces your poem to move in directions you may not have considered.

NOVEMBER

19

. . . .

Multisyllabic Words And
The Compassion They Show

Richard Hugo wrote in his book *The Triggering Town*, "With multisyllabic words we can show compassion, tenderness, and tranquility." Write a poem that has more multisyllabic words than single syllabic words and see how that changes your tone and content. The poem can be about anything you wish, but if you're stuck, begin the poem with the line: *Another beginning of unexpected...* and see where it goes.

NOVEMBER

20

. . . .

Small Talk

Write a poem that seems to be only about small talk, but allow some important information or discussion into this poem. Allow the conversation to move into some challenging territory and see how the characters in your poem react—do they continue discussing the weather after someone mentions they've had an affair or do they move into this topic? Write the poem in first person as if you are a participant in the conversation or in third person, as if you're watching this happen from the corner of the room.

NOVEMBER

21

. . . .

No Good Stories Come From
"After We Ate A Salad"

Write a poem that begins *After three glasses of wine* or *After three shots of whiskey,* and continue writing about the antics that follow. Allow your imagination to take you into the world of people who have lost their inhibitions. See what they say or what they do after the alcohol has been consumed.

NOVEMBER

22

. . . .

Second Person, This One's For You

Write a poem to the "You." It can be the world "you,"
the American "you," or directly to a specific person,
including yourself. Use three of your favorite words as
well as words that contain an "oo" sound, like *tune, blue,
soon.*

NOVEMBER

23

. . . .

That's A Negative

Write a poem that uses more negatives than positives. Use words like *no, can't, nope, anti, negative.* Write the poem about something you like but can't have. Feel free to use repetition to highlight the negative words as needed.

NOVEMBER

24

. . . .

Old Flame

Write a poem about something you did with an old
boyfriend or girlfriend that you've never forgotten. If
you could do it again, what would you do differently?
Add what you would do differently to the poem, along
with the words *hot sauce* just for fun.

NOVEMBER

25

· ·

Dear Fill-In-The-Blank

Write an experimental poem to all the things in your life
that you either worry about, are afraid of, or events that
have shaken you up. Allow the repetition of "dear" to
guide you—*Dear Airplane Ride, Dear Elevator, Dear
Skyscraper whose windows never seemed strong enough…*

. . . .

But At Least There Was
Pumpkin Pie

Write a poem about something going wrong at a Thanksgiving dinner. The event can be something very major or something minor, such as an oven catching fire or two guests in a fight over the wishbone. Include images of Thanksgiving in the poem—the specific foods eaten to what is on TV.

NOVEMBER

27

. . . .

She Gives Me Love, Crazy Love

Write a love poem where you don't mention love, hugs, kisses, sex, or touching. Allow the feeling of love to emerge from the actions of the characters or images that you choose. For extra credit, have the poem be about two people who shouldn't love each other, such as a couple divorced for ten years or a married man and a married woman.

NOVEMBER

28

. . . .

Geography

Write a poem that explores geography in a fresh way. Think geography of the body or the geography of a rhubarb. Let your imagination and boundaries go and see what you end up with. Feel free to use any words that have to do with geography of the world—*continent, country, ocean, equator, Prime Meridian,* etc.—in your poem.

NOVEMBER

29

· ·

First Words

Write a poem that begins with the next thing anyone says to you. If you're alone and there's no one around, either call up a friend or turn on the radio and use the first thing you hear as an opening line.

. . . .

Mark Twain And Tom Sawyer

Mark Twain was born today in 1810. Write a poem
that includes Mark Twain or one of his characters,
along with a pipe, clawfoot bathtub, and a raft. The
poem can be about anything, but if it includes a
mysterious treasure or someone painting a white picket
fence, you get extra credit.

DECEMBER

DECEMBER

1

• •

Scrabble

On this day in 1948, the popular board game *Scrabble* was copyright registered. Write a poem with as many two and three letter words as possible. Examples: *ax, yo, ho, ox, us, up, ho, id, in, us, up, act, age, ago, aid, auk, ark, boa, rex, qat, pox, pow, paw, peg, yak, yam, yap.*

DECEMBER

2

. . . .

Chanukah

During the darkest, coldest part of the year, religious festivals, such as Chanukah, bring light, warmth, and hope into our lives. Write a poem celebrating the miracle of light in a dark and gloomy landscape. For instance, the traditions of lighting candles, stringing lights on bushes, and sitting around a crackling fire. For added inspiration, read Dylan Thomas' poem "Light Breaks When No Sun Shines":

http://www.poets.org/viewmedia.php/prmMID/ 15380

DECEMBER

3

∴∴∴∴∴∴∴∴∴∴∴∴∴∴∴∴∴∴∴∴∴∴∴

Cosmic

On this date in 1621, Galileo Galilee unveiled his
rendition of the telescope. Point your pen to the
heavens today, addressing the discovery of Io, Europa,
Ganymede, and Callisto, the largest moons of Jupiter.
Write your poem in the form of a letter in the voice of
Galileo explaining to all of humanity that celestial
bodies orbit around planets, not just Earth. Extra
credit: address the letter to the Catholic Church, which
finally declared in 1992 that Galileo's conviction and
imprisonment were an "error."

DECEMBER

4

. . . .

You Must Change Your Life

In celebration of Rainier Maria Rilke's birthday, write a poem inspired by "Archaic Torso of Apollo." This poem is based on a supposition that the seeing power of the eyes, though no longer attached to the statue by way of the head, persist. Write a poem that makes a case for something or someone missing having the power to effect change in the viewer. Rilke's poem is available at the Academy of American Poets website:

http:www.poets.org/viewmedia.php/prmMID/158 14

DECEMBER

5

. . . .

Glosa

The glosa is an early Renaissance form developed in the 14th and 15th centuries by poets in the Spanish court. In a glosa, tribute is paid to another poet. The opening quatrain, the cabeza, is written by someone else. Each of these four lines will be repeated consecutively as the 10th line of each of four stanzas. Each stanza "glosses" (interprets, explains) the borrowed text. Optionally, each stanza's 6th, 9th and 10th lines rhyme. A great example is Diane Suess's "Ring of Fire Glosa":
http://www.unsplendid.com/5/1/5-1_seuss_ring_frames.htm

DECEMBER

6

· ·

Hip Haiku

Try writing some haiku that resist being about apple
blossoms, insects, or frogs. Instead use the 5/7/5
syllables in a series of three-line poems that deal with
subjects such as bad hair, infectious diseases, or people
who've never heard of Rumi.

DECEMBER

7

. . . .

To-Do List

Write a poem in the form of a to-do list, preferably a to-do list of a famous literary figure. What would Henry David Thoreau have on his to-do list? How about Gustav Flaubert? Perhaps Emily Dickinson's to-do list would include practicing her scales, writing a letter, baking ginger cake, ironing her white dress, identifying wildflowers, witnessing a funeral, and quarreling with her sisters or brother. You will likely need to spend some time to get the order of your list just right, saving the best for last. Your poem may be humorous or grave/poignant.

DECEMBER

8

. . . .

Letter To An Abstract Noun

Begin a poem "Dear Time" or "Dear Eternity" but instead of continuing in the realm of abstraction, make your letter specific and concrete. Perhaps you are unhappy with these concepts. Voice your opposition! If you get stuck, include one or more of the following words in your letter: *skin, geography, regret, tugboat, pudding, fibrous, pumice.*

DECEMBER

9

. . . .

Help Me Rondeau

The rondeau is a lyric poem originating in 13th century France, popular among medieval court poets and musicians. Named after the French word for "round," the rondeau is characterized by the repeating lines of the *rentrement,* or refrain, and the two rhyme sounds throughout. Traditionally the form devoted itself to emotional subjects such as spiritual worship, courtship, romance, and the melancholy that morphed into a *c'est la vie* attitude. Rondeaus are composed of fifteen lines, eight to ten syllables each, divided stanzaically into a quintet, a quatrain, and a sestet. The *rentrement* consists of the first few words or the entire first line of the first stanza, recurring as the last line of both the second and third stanzas. The rhyme scheme is aabba aabR aabbaR. See more about the rondeau at:

www.poets.org/viewmedia.php/prmMID/5789#st hash.VUzarroF.dpuf

DECEMBER

10

· ·

Fame Is A Fickle Food

Emily Dickinson, whose birthday is today, wrote *Fame is a fickle food / upon a shifting plate.* Write a poem that defines what fame is, how one should go about achieving it, and what happens once one has it. Feel free to choose a different image besides food and allow that to act as a larger metaphor.

DECEMBER

11

. . . .

Shoe Poem

On this date in 1900, Ronald McFeeley obtained a patent for a shoemaking machine. Celebrate with an ode to a shoe or pair of shoes. For inspiration, head to your shoe bin or recall favorite shoes that you no longer own, listing and describing them, along with places you've walked in each pair. Spend some time describing the beat-up hiking boots that walked a section of the Pacific Crest Trail in 1999, or the sandals you wore as you explored the Latin Quarter of Paris for the first time. Your poem may end up focusing on one pair of shoes, or pay tribute to a year, decade, or lifetime of walking.

DECEMBER

12

· ·

When Wisdom Knocks

Write a poem that begins with a wise person visiting you (Socrates, Eleanor Roosevelt, Indira Gandhi, Marie Curie, Lao Tzu). What do you talk about? What do you serve him/her for dinner? Where is s/he going to sleep? If you have questions, now is the time to ask.

DECEMBER

13

. . . .

Writing James Wright

In honor of James Wright's birthday, write an ode to a natural object in the spirit of his "To the Saguaro Cactus Tree in the Desert Rain." Wright states that he wishes he were *the spare shadow of the roadrunner* or *the tear the tarantula weeps*. Share in your poem which parts of specific animals you would like to be, something you hate, and at least one thing you would never do. Wright's poem can be found here:

http://www.poets.org/viewmedia.php/prmMID/20942

DECEMBER

14

. . . .

Carnival

On this date in 1926, the Tilt-a-Whirl trademark was registered. In honor of this invention, write a poem that shares your favorite amusement park memories. Think back to when you were a kid or the time you took your own child to the carnival. Did you ride in a giant teacup or float above the crowd on a winged elephant? Share your carnival memories vividly and honestly in your poem today.

DECEMBER

15

. . . .

No More Masks!

In honor of Muriel Rukeyser, born this day in 1913, compose a poem inspired by "The Poem As Mask." As you write, veer away from your usual fallback words, subject matter, and/or themes, and instead share head-on about a difficult memory or time of great personal anguish. Rukeyser's poem can be found here:

http://www.poets.org/viewmedia.php/prmMID/16695

DECEMBER

16

Mall Visit

Visit a mall, taking notes about what you hear, smell, see, and taste. Jot down overheard bits of conversation, brand names, and descriptions of the people shopping. Use these notes as fodder for a poem about shopping for gifts and consider the overabundance of material items in some regions of the world.

DECEMBER

17

. . . .

What Would Mr. Brady Say?

On this date in 1989, *The Simpsons* debuted on national television. Write a poem in the voice of a famous TV personality. Whether it's Bart Simpson or Alice from *The Brady Bunch*, put your character in a compelling, potentially comic situation. Example: Mrs. June Cleaver decides to go to clown college.

DECEMBER

18

. . . .

The Receptionist

Most of us have had the experience of visiting a barber or hairstylist and telling him or her something very personal we could never tell a friend, spouse, or parent. For today, imagine that you are sitting in a hair salon, telling your trusted stylist a long-guarded secret. Now write a poem from the point of view of the receptionist who overhears you.

DECEMBER

19

. . . .

This I Believe

Are you for or against getaway weekends in Vegas? Do you believe wolves should be reintroduced in the western US? What's your idea of a perfect day? Write a credo poem that shares the core beliefs that guide your actions.

DECEMBER

20

. . . .

Tell Me What You Want

Write a poem in the form of a letter enumerating your wishes and desires. You might want to include why you wish for each item on your list. For comic effect, juxtapose obtainable wishes (a rowboat) with less obtainable ones (world peace).

DECEMBER

21

· ·

Darkness

In celebration of the winter solstice, write a poem that begins *96% of the universe is made up of the dark and unknown...* Your poem might posit what is the other 4% made of or perhaps share (with specific images) why you enjoy (or don't enjoy) winter.

DECEMBER

22

· ·

In Praise Of The Return Of Light

Many feel that the best thing about the winter solstice is that the days can get no shorter, as for the next six months they will lengthen with each passing day. In celebration of this turn toward brightness, write a short poem about the return of light where objects like stars, lamps, and candles burn bright. For further inspiration, see Mark Strand's poem "The Coming of Light": http://www.poets.org/viewmedia.php/prmMID/16327

DECEMBER

23

· ·

Robert Bly's Advice

In celebration of Robert Bly's birthday, choose an
animal and have it advise the reader how he or she
should live. Examples: a beaver cautions about the
building of dams, a squirrel has something to say about
hoarding. Begin your poem: *I don't want to frighten you,
but...* For further inspiration, listen to Bly's "Advice
from the Geese":

http://www.poets.org/viewmedia.php/prmMID/
20027

DECEMBER

24

. . . .

In The Beginning

Write a poem today using one of these opening lines:

Beneath the moon I saw...
Because the day was rushed...
In my pocket I keep...
Some days disappear like...
At the party s/he discovered...
I want to be more like the color red...

For extra credit, write a six stanza poem in which each of the above opening lines begins a stanza.

DECEMBER

25

. . . .

Merry Haiku

Write three haiku today: one about a Christmas tree lot, the second about a miniature train set, and the third about a visiting relative you don't often see. Do not force a connection between the three haiku, but create one title for all three.

DECEMBER

26

· ·

Universe

"You can see everything in the universe in one tangerine," states Thich Nhat Hanh. Choose a type of fruit and write a poem about how it does and doesn't resemble the cosmos. Feel free to draw from the vocabulary of astronomy to help your poem along.

DECEMBER

27

. . . .

Hey, Mr. Spaceman

Imagine that you are an alien visiting planet Earth, trying to make sense of our customs, our high regard for machines and technology. What would a person from another planet make of us? What would an alien think of us as we walk down the street staring into our smart phones? Share your reactions to our strange behaviors in a poem written in the persona of a visitor from outer space.

DECEMBER

28

· ·

Favorite Childhood Food

Write a poem about a favorite food from childhood: *vanilla milk shakes, French fries, dill pickles, watermelon soda,* etc. Who did you eat this beloved type of food with? Where were you living? Who were your friends?

DECEMBER

29

. . . .

Palm Poem

Today's assignment is to write a poem inspired by the lines on the palm of your hand. Imagine you are consulting a fortune teller. What future events does she foresee and what shocking information does she tell you? For extra credit, rename the lines of your hand. Perhaps the life line can become the "fly-by-the-seat-of-your-pants" line or the heart line can become the "twice-divorced" line.

DECEMBER

30

. . . .

Ingredients List

Make a list of the foods you need in order to make a real or imagined feast: *pomegranates, grenadine, cinnamon, saffron, lo mein noodles*, etc. Write a long, skinny poem that focuses on the ingredients themselves, with minimal commentary or explanation.

DECEMBER

31

. . . .

Making Light Of Taking Stock

Begin by freewriting a list of memorable events of the past year: places you traveled, people you met, books you read, etc. Then, take the true and earnest statements about these events, and embellish and exaggerate them until they are funny. Example: on your trip to Florida you may have actually seen two people wielding metal detectors, but in your poem, the entire coastline will be covered with folks out there medal detecting. Create a poem that both preserves some of the highlights of your year and leaves you (and hopefully your reader) smiling.

About The Authors

Kelli Russell Agodon is the author of four books of poems: *Hourglass Museum, Letters from the Emily Dickinson Room* (Winner of the ForeWord Magazine Book of the Year Prize in Poetry and Finalist for the Washington State Book Award,) *Small Knots,* and the chapbook, *Geography.* She also co-edited the first eBook anthology of contemporary women's poetry, *Fire On Her Tongue.* Connect with her at www.facebook.com/agodon or visit her homepage at: www.agodon.com

Martha Silano is the author of four poetry collections, including the Saturnalia Books Poetry Prize winning *The Little Office of the Immaculate Conception*, an Academy of American Poets Noted Book of 2011 and finalist for the Washington State Book Award, and *Reckless Lovely*, also from Saturnalia. She is poetry editor of *Crab Creek Review* and teaches creative writing and composition at Bellevue College. Martha blogs at Blue Positive: http://bluepositive.blogspot.com/

Notes

Made in the USA
San Bernardino, CA
15 October 2015